Life Is Great,
Even When It Sucks

Life Is Great, Even When It Sucks

What Makes People Do the Things They Do

Ellen Nyland

Copyright © 2015 by Ellen Nyland.

Library of Congress Control Number:	2015904029
ISBN: Hardcover	978-1-5035-5267-8
Softcover	978-1-4990-1419-8
eBook	978-1-5035-5266-1

All rights reserved. No part of this book may be reproduced or transmitted in any form or by any means, electronic or mechanical, including photocopying, recording, or by any information storage and retrieval system, without permission in writing from the copyright owner.

All charts, tables and images in the book are all author's creation.

All names used in the book are changed for privacy reasons.

Print information available on the last page.

Rev. date: 08/18/2015

To order additional copies of this book, contact:
Xlibris
1-888-795-4274
www.Xlibris.com
Orders@Xlibris.com
625850

CONTENTS

Acknowledgments vii
Introduction ix

Chapter 1:   I am who I am 1
Chapter 2:   Trust 22
Chapter 3:   Conflict 51
Chapter 4:   Accountability 78
Chapter 5:   Commitment 110
Chapter 6:   Result 142
Chapter 7:   Family Cultures 170
Chapter 8:   Societal Cultures 188
Chapter 9:   Love 210
Chapter 10: Steps You Can Take 235
Chapter 11: Rewards and Reactions 266

Conclusion 291
Appendix A My Life Story 303
Appendix B Real-Life Stories 325
Appendix C Values Questionnaire 344

ACKNOWLEDGMENTS

To write these acknowledgments is no small task. Everybody has contributed to this book. Even you, reader because you are part of the human race, and I was inspired by you. Thank you.

First and foremost, I give my great gratitude to God. Your silent encouragement and insights were incredibly valuable.

To my husband, Luke; father-in-law Jan and previous employers, Will and Sue, I thank you for showing me unconditional love, so I could teach it to others. To my family, who showed me the impact that beliefs have on your life, I thank you.

Marike, Annerieke, Joost and Steve, all of you helped me organize my thoughts on paper. Great thanks to my sister, Marike, whose support was of priceless value. Without you, I never would have had the courage to write this book. All our conversations and comparing notes are woven into this book. Great thanks to Annerieke and Laura for creating the cover and to Heather, my graphic designer, for making my book look so amazing. I thank Jozien, Joost, and Marike for being so courageous in sharing your life stories. I know you will inspire many people.

Thank you to everyone who filled out my survey. You brought insight and life experience to the book. To all the people who showed the world their **I Am status**—Jesus, Dr. Martin Luther King Jr., Nelson Mandela, and Mother Theresa, to name a few—who you were and what you did continues to greatly inspire us all.

I want to give thanks for all the life experiences I've had. Without those, I couldn't have written this book. They made me who I am now.

INTRODUCTION

Every day of our lives we face old and new challenges. How we deal with them depends on our state of mind. Often situations will trigger our subconscious belief systems into action. That action can vary from compassion to hateful thoughts toward another person or oneself.

Since I was a little girl, I've wondered, "What makes people do the things they do?" I've lived with four generations on one farm, emigrated to a new country, raised a family and am a Certified Professional Co-Active Coach, trained at The Coaches Training Institute in San Rafael, California. I've discovered by observing my clients and the people around me that the answer to my question goes deeper than people's behavior in everyday interactions.

What can look like you lashing out at another, in reality, can be nothing more than being so focused on getting something done that you don't pay attention to what you say and how you say it. Out of love, we may try to protect someone against what we think is a threat. In reality, we are saying, "I don't trust you to make the right decision for yourself."

Of course it is not always this black and white. Every situation has a unique foundation, even when it doesn't look that way. Is it any wonder that there is so much misunderstanding, hurt, and conflict everywhere in the world? The question to ask ourselves is, "How we can change the situation."

To change the world, start with yourself. Although overused, this is a core truth. I found that out for myself. When I started my observation of human interaction, I realized that we **all** are magnificent. We have this beautiful inner light that shines so brightly, it almost blinds us.

I call this your **I Am status**.

When I say everybody has it, I mean everybody. It does not shine in only a chosen few. Even people we believe are rude, anti-social or criminals have an **I Am status**. Everybody we interact with, in one way or another, has an **I Am status**.

If everyone has one, then how come we don't always see this light in our daily lives? The answer is simple and complex, at the same time. We are all influenced by these factors:

- ✓ We learn from what we see, smell, taste, hear, and touch.
- ✓ Our experiences guide how we make decisions.
- ✓ Children look to the adults in their lives for guidance on what is acceptable and what is the social norm.
- ✓ Globally, all societies are built on rules about how to trust, how to handle conflict, how to be accountable, how to be committed, and the results of these actions.
- ✓ This five-point system is always filled with insecurity by the people who use it — all of us.
- ✓ We experience life and the world from our personal points of view.
- ✓ It is very tough to view life from somebody else's perspective. We aren't taught how.

Life events, family culture, societal culture, global culture, and media culture play a role in how we learn the five-point system and contribute to the insecurity it is based on. This system is just the beginning of understanding the core question, "What makes people do the things they do?"

Are you confused?

No need. We will dive into every aspect I mentioned. When you put the separate layers on top of each other and mix them all together, it is impossible to detect what behavior is coming from where. It is no wonder our **I Am status** gets buried under all the superficial stuff and is difficult to find and use in our daily lives.

Does that mean that we are doomed to life in the dark?

Absolutely not. It is your choice whether you want to live in the dark or in the light. You are in control of this, nobody else. You are the only one who can dust off your light and make it shine.

Sure a great coach, therapist or minister can help you, but ultimately you are the only one who can do it. In this book I will present steps you can take to bring you to your light. I promise you they work.

My clients, some of my friends, family and clients use the same strategies I will show you consistently. They find life feels lighter, more true to who they are. They feel more confident, and don't take everything so personally. They do the best they can and want the same for everybody else.

The work you do, using the personal steps I show you may be messy, heartrending and difficult, but with them you will be able to leap the hurdles that have always kept you from being who you really are. The rewards will be bigger than you can even imagine.

I understand that you may think this sound too good to be true. That's why I asked a couple of people to let me share their life stories and have also included my own story — to show you that although life is not always a bed of roses, with the right tools you can get through the times that suck without losing who you are.

These stories, our stories demonstrate the amazing resilience of the human race, if you dare take a good look at your own life and the lives of the people close to you. This will help you to walk in others' shoes more easily, and hopefully you will become less judgmental of others and yourself.

By being less judgmental you will no longer be a prisoner to all your outside influences. When you finish this book and have done your best at completing the various steps, I hope and pray that you too will say, "Life is great even when it sucks."

CHAPTER 1

I am who I am

As we have the courage to examine our personal insecurities, beliefs, and values, we will find our **I Am status,** that unique toolbox of traits we possess and will understand its power for change.

To help you with this journey, I will share my experiences with this journey and how tapping into my **I Am status** made my life more glorious, less rattled and more manageable, without losing contact with the people around me.

On this path you will encounter your inner demons and those of the people around you. This is your hero's journey. The result will empower you to find the miracles and courage to be who you were born to be.

You aren't alone on this path. More people than you know are on the same journey. To find them ask yourself, "Which person has positively influenced my life?"

Whether this person is still alive and close to you or with you in memory, the imprint they leave on you lies inside you. That's where you will be doing your work. It helps to find like-minded people for company and support, especially when roadblocks crop up. Keep in mind, supporting is different from enabling.

To bring more clarity on the difficulties we are dealing with I will explain the five-point system one segment at a time and then discuss the influences family, societal, and media cultures have on your **I Am status**. I will also give you exercises for finding and strengthening the contents of your toolbox. By doing this you will experience the miracle of you as you truly are.

Surrounded by Miracles

When I look around me, I am amazed by the world, all of its aspects, nature, technology, and human behavior. A flower, a quote I read, or a face on the street puts me in awe.

When you pay attention to the world around you, what you see is its beauty and the miracle of life in action. The first leaves in the spring, the smell of fresh-cut grass, or the first snowfall can give you the magical feeling of awe and wonder.

How is this possible, and how does all this coexist on one planet? I see miracles happen every day because

I look for them. We can all experience miracles, if we look for them.

...and Mysteries

But nothing fascinates me more than human interaction. I can't explain my fascination with it. I struggled for the longest time with the question, "What makes people do the things they do?" As a small child, I saw people say one thing and do something different. I was surprised by the things they said and the judgments they made. There was a disconnect.

At times, watching people and their actions, I have asked myself, where did the human race go wrong? Is this planet still worth living on? If I watch the news and reality shows, what I see portrayed is scary and negative. The world, sometimes, appears to be a living hell.

Surrounded by negative messages, it is easy to get discouraged. Why do our best? It doesn't seem to matter. How can we change the big picture? If we do our best, somebody else will cut us off at the knees, just to make sure we fail. It appears hopeless.

Many of us feel this way and on the surface, that feeling appears justified. We have a tendency to put each other down, just to make ourselves look better. We deal with envy by judging people, motivated by the fear that the next person will have more success than we do, and therefore have a higher status. But if we look deeper when asking, "What makes people do the things they do?" we find very different and unique answers.

The human race is not a faceless group of strangers you pass in the street. The human race is you and me, our partners, children, neighbors and coworkers. Every face you see every day from the person who serves you at the restaurant and store, the person who drives in front of you on the road, the drivers who cut you off in traffic, the teacher of your children, the officer who gives you a speeding ticket, or the border security officer who asks you a million questions are all part of the human race.

I-Am Status

What do they all have in common, and what makes them different? Each person, all of us, shares the following common qualities:

- ✓ We all have feelings.
- ✓ We are all born with a magnificent **I Am status** (qualities that form our authentic self).
- ✓ We all have dreams.
- ✓ We all know what we know.
- ✓ We have all been taught the five-point system.

- ✓ We all react to the events in life in the way we have learned from others around us.
- ✓ We all adapt to our environment.
- ✓ We all have insecurities.

What makes us different?
- ✓ The life experiences we have.
- ✓ Our perspective on life.
- ✓ The way we are taught the five-point system.
- ✓ How we adapt to our environment.
- ✓ How we express our insecurities.
- ✓ Our **I Am status** - the toolbox we are born with.

I'm not talking about differences in race, sexual orientation, culture, or religion. When you strip those away, the differences dwindle down to the short list mentioned above.

Those differences make us who we are. And it is our **I Am status**, the toolbox we carry within us that form who we will always be.

The terms toolbox and **I Am status** are used throughout the book. These two terms refer to the most precious thing you will ever own. Your **I Am status** and your toolbox describe the traits and qualities you are born with. They are unique to you. Nobody can give them to you, nor can you buy them. Most important of all, nobody can take them away from you.

Your **I Am status** is your core - the foundation and the building blocks that you brought with you when you came into this world that makes you unique, a miracle. You are who you are. That is your **I Am status**. To make it real to yourself, use a mirror and look yourself in the eye and tell yourself, "I am who I am."

Have you ever really looked at a newborn baby? If you have, you've seen the core of that child, in its purest form. Babies don't know yet how to hide behind masks. They haven't learned the five-point system. They do not possess the art of pretending, yet. Babies show their greatness, their light without trying. Babies are magnificent to those who really look and see them. There is no shame, blame, guilt or judgment in a baby's eyes. There is only love in the most precious, nonjudgmental way. All babies possess that ability to be purely who they are.

That is why each baby is so unique, even identical twins. Their uniqueness lies in the presence of their **I Am status** that lies open for the entire world to see, if one truly looks. From birth, the wonderful, strong qualities we are born with are there.

To survive and thrive in this world, we need a solid set of values and principles to help us deal with the life events that come our way. When we look at babies, we see the various qualities they are born with that make each of them, and therefore us, unique. Nobody is born with exactly the same toolbox. This becomes clear when you look at large families. Despite having the same parents, the same gene pool and growing up within the same environment, none of the children are the same.

Bottom Line: Our only similarity is that we all have an I Am status, a toolbox but we are different due to the qualities and traits that are in born into each person's toolbox - We are, who we are.

Teaching the Five-Point System

Going back to the beginning of life, the moment a baby is born, the baby trusts that we won't hurt them and will protect them from harm. Babies depend on us for their care and protection. They did not ask to be born. When we took actions that resulted in their birth, we committed to looking after them, for as long as they need us.

In return, babies give us unconditional love, and let us know in their own way what they need. As they grow under our care, they reflect back to us what we have taught them.

The five-point system is what parents teach their children. It centers on how children are taught to trust (trust), deal with conflict (conflict), be accountable (accountability), commit (commitment), and get results (results). What appears clear and simple becomes confusing and fraught with misunderstandings when mixed with their parents' life experiences.

The challenge in teaching anyone is that we tend to teach from our own perspective. We don't consider the person we are teaching. We teach others from our toolbox, our view on life, our circumstances, our failures, and our own personal fears instead of modifying our teaching to the toolbox of the individual we are teaching.

This tendency may be the core reason for all conflict in the world. But for now, let's examine how the perspective of others influences the way we learn the five-point system of our initial education.

People know what they know—no more, no less. Your core attitude to life is part of who you are (I Am What I Am) before you are even born.

As parents begin to teach their children, using their outlook and experience, they create a family culture, that at the same time is influenced by and influencing society's culture. In the Appendix A, is my life story to demonstrate how my family's experience influenced the way I was taught he five-point system.

Considering that from birth until adulthood, we are being taught the five-point system, is it any wonder many of us feel as we do. How difficult it must be for our **I Am status** to blossom? Most of us don't even know that we have a core toolbox or that we need to cultivate it to experience a more fulfilling life.

All of us encounter difficult challenges in life, and many of them suck. But those challenges give us opportunities to cultivate and strengthen our toolbox. It all depends on our perspective and the choices we make on our personal journeys.

Life is more complicated than we think. For example, due to not being able to afford a post-secondary education, my dad had a low-paying job. When I was a child, Dad attended night school to get ahead in his career, but he had to quit because money was tight. He had four children to raise and responsibilities.

Mom had a talent for making a quarter into a dollar. We never went hungry, and we always had clean, tidy clothes on our backs. We didn't make a big deal out of this because the people in our neighborhood were in the same position.

We had a very traditional family. Mom looked after the children, and Dad was the provider. Dad spent his time either working or volunteering for different organizations. Sometimes he was so busy, I didn't think he knew I was alive.

Let's take a step back, and look at the bigger picture. Here is a man who was very smart but with a low-paying job. How much self-esteem do you think he had?

To compensate for his lack of education and status in this career, he channeled his knowledge into volunteer positions that gave no monetary rewards. They cost him money, which tightened the family budget and stressed Mom. A circle of grief was created.

This is all true, but you know what is also true? Dad was on first-name basis with a prime minister of The Netherlands. He was in the inner office of the Pope twice, and he helped to save a factory from closure. That company is still in business after thirty years.

Those are achievements I sometimes forget, when dealing with the grief I experienced as a child. My father's intelligence and drive for positive change is who he is.

It is difficult to focus on what someone does well, and not the negative way they impact you. How often do we criticize instead of compliment others? How often do you criticize yourself, instead of being proud of all you've accomplished? We are our own worst critics.

We get so focused on hiding our insecurities that we forget to cultivate our strengths. We don't accept the life we have. We are unhappy because we are not living the life we want.

Where do our insecurities come from?

We see them most clearly in the people close to us. We don't recognize them as insecurities but see them as the truth in life. When we are small, we think that our parents know everything. We don't realize that they are hiding their personal insecurities behind masks of confidence and authority. By the time we realize this, the damage is already done. Some of their insecurities have become our own.

That's why you will see certain characteristic traits in the same family. We have a choice about how we learn the five-point system. We always have a choice about how we look at and experience a life event. The first step is to be aware of that choice. That should be the main thing we teach children. Unfortunately, it is often the truth we have to learn on our own.

For example, when I was three years old, my mom took me to a family up the street and introduced me to their daughter, Mieke. At the time I could not have foreseen that the family and Mieke would become my safe haven. God really does gives you what you need in life, even when you don't recognize it.

Mieke and I could play for hours on end without fighting. At that time, Mieke was an only child, so all the attention went to her and to me. In my family, I was just one of four kids and my Mom had a lot of housework to do. There was not much one-on-one attention for each of us.

But when my siblings and I came home from school, Mom was always waiting with tea and cookies. She encouraged us to talk about our days as she cooked, did laundry or sewed. When I look back, I think that my mom was doing more hearing than listening.

Three Stages of Listening

We rarely teach or show our children the art of listening. Children know the difference between when you are just hearing what they say and when you are listening. So do adults. When somebody is totally listening to you, you feel the difference.

When we are really listened to, we feel connected, understood, heard, valuable, and important.

When somebody just hears and their mind is busy with other things, we feel we aren't important enough and that what we say can be dismissed.

I've learned that most people only hear and do not know the difference. The skill of listening is an art few try to master. As a society we need to become more aware of the art of listening.

How good are your listening skills? At the Coaches Training Institute (CTI), where they train and certify people to become life coaches, I learned there were three levels of listening.

- ✓ Level 1—Internal Listening
    With internal listening you are focused on yourself. You hear the words that are spoken, but your attention is on what those words mean for you personally. It is all about your thoughts, feelings, judgments, and how what is being said impacts you.

This level of listening is necessary for tasks like shopping by yourself. You have shopping to complete and you have to pay attention to where you are going so that you don't run into anybody. When finished, you need to hear how much you owe. The focus on yourself is appropriate at this time. There are many scenarios where Level 1 listening is useful.

- ✓ Level 2—Focused Listening
    Focused listening is all about the other person. You and your conversation partner are so focused on each other that you are not aware of anything that goes on around you. You pick up your conversational partner's emotions and tone of voice. You hear what the person is not saying. When you listen on this level, you are not attached to your own agenda. You mirror your thoughts to each other.

This is very powerful in a business setting and in personal conversation. Most business deals go sour when the negotiating parties are not focused on the deal and on what the other party is truly saying. Personal conversations often turn into a fight when people are not paying attention to what is being said, with both words and body language. Subconsciously we create the impression that we are superior to the other party, when in reality all parties are just listening at Level 1.

✓ Level 3—Global Listening
Global listening is listening with all your senses, as if every pore of your body is tuned into the conversation. You hear your partner's voice but also the environment around you.

For example, when you meet a friend on the street, and you start talking, you know you are listening at Level 3 when you notice the noise of the cars passing, people coming by you, and the smell of the hotdog stand ten meters away. You will also know when your friend needs to go because she is getting cold, just by looking at her body language.

All this you notice because you are totally engaged in the conversation with your friend. When you start listening at Level 3, you strengthen your intuition muscles. If you are very intuitive, you are already listening at Level 3 most of the time. At this level of listening you give the recipient the feeling of importance and sense of being heard. You also pick up on clues that help you see what is really being said.

This is one of the biggest gifts you can give someone, the feeling of being understood (even when you don't agree with them), of being heard and of being important to the person who is listening to you.

What happens when you are only heard, not actively listened to? I have always been a sensitive person, and four years ago one of my teachers in leadership told me that I live in Level 3 listening all the time. It dawned on me that as a child I never felt heard unless at Mieke's place.

In the midst of our busy household I felt alone and out of place. I had the feeling that nobody understood me and that I was not important enough to spend energy on. Now I know that was not done intentionally.

It was simply me listening at Level 3 when the rest of my family was listening at Level 1. The difference created confusion and misunderstanding about who I was in the family. I absorbed these feelings before the age of five.

Curiosity and Miracles

When my brother Carl was born, my life changed radically. Carl was born with spina bifida. The doctors informed my parents that Carl could die or be paralyzed from the neck down. Over the next five years Mom went to the hospital at least once or twice at week for one doctor's appointment or another.

My first experience with a miracle was my bother Carl. We were told Carl would not have any quality of life, but it turned out that he not only survived but thrived, which is a miracle. The only thing Carl can't do to this day is curl his left hand inward. He is a fully functioning, well-loved man.

You need to start recognizing that wonderful things happen, even in devastating times. Your **I Am status** can recognize those miracles, you just need to be open to seeing wonders, you formerly viewed as ordinary.

A client once told me that he wished he'd seen and experienced such miracles after hearing my stories. I told him, "John, please look into your life, and you tell me about your miracles. You have to look first and pay attention, and then you will find them."

Most of us believe that miracles are only those written in the Bible or other holy books. We see miracles as huge events that make the news. Those are miracles, but there are many more every day, less obvious ones.

For example, it's a miracle to have no worries about where your next meal will come from, to be warm on a cold winter day, to see a flower growing and blooming in an impossible place, to watch the furious and magnificent power of a storm from a safe place, to gaze upon a loved one sleeping, to live in a peaceful country, and to be loved unconditionally by a pet.

When I was nine years old, I discovered a puppy under a car on our street. Nobody in our neighborhood had puppies or was missing one, so where this pup came from was a mystery. The moment I found this pup I fell in love with her and she with me.

We named her Fanny, and she followed me around everywhere. Then Mom decided that we couldn't keep

Fanny, she gave her to my aunt, who lived two streets away from us. I went to see Fanny as much as I could. Fanny always chose me over my aunt's family.

One day Fanny was hit by a car and killed. I was devastated. I prayed to have one moment to properly say good-bye to Fanny for five years. My prayer was heard.

When I was fourteen, for Christmas I asked for a Fanny dog. Now Fanny was not a purebred dog; she was a mixed breed. My family didn't know what to do.

My brother, Case, went on a dog hunt. After much searching (this was before the Internet), he found a litter of pups. When he went to see them, his jaw dropped. In this litter was a dog exactly like Fanny. I have a picture of Fanny and a picture of this second dog, Elke, and you can't tell the difference.

It was the best Christmas ever. I loved Elke. She was my everything for eleven years. She knew all my secrets, my happy moments and she never left my side. I'm tearing up now, just writing about her.

Another example of an everyday miracle in my life was when my brother, Harry, worked a summer job, and with the money he earned he bought me a new bike.

How many brothers would do that? He stepped in when my parents didn't have the money, because I needed a bike to get to school. His act of selflessness showed me the importance of family and of having each other's back with no-strings attached. Situations like this show the kind of impression we can make on others in our lives.

With the experience of being the recipient of an act of love, it was and still is easier to do the same for somebody else. I can do this because somebody else taught me, with their actions, the importance of such gestures.

In our busy lives we often fail to notice incredible acts of kindness shown to us. We take them for granted and fail to the thank the giver. Instead we give more importance and focus to the drama and violence around us. We rarely acknowledge miracles, because we haven't been taught and shown the definition of a miracle.

To begin seeing small miracles, take a look at your hands and really observe them for a moment. Ask yourself, "What did I do today with them? How are they working for me?" Look at how perfectly the skin covers the bones and muscles.

Our hands work seemingly effortlessly. Do this mental exercise with everyday objects and discover the beauty in everything. Rediscover the world we miss, by stopping and really looking around you. Stop mistaking the common for the miraculous.

Search every day for miracles. Keep a list. Explore your surroundings as a toddler does by feeling, tasting, seeing, and touching everything. This is their way of discovering the world, and everything they see is a miracle.

> Miracles rest not so much upon healing power coming suddenly near us from afar but upon our perceptions being made finer, so that, for the moment, our eyes can see and our ears can hear what has been around us always.
>
> —Willa Cather, Death Comes for the Archbishop

The biggest gift we can give ourselves is to never lose that wonder and curiosity and to keep asking millions of questions. As parents, we discourage this early tendency because we are so focused on teaching things from our own perspective, which is the result of our parents' teachings and their parents' teachings. We don't focus on our children's **I Am status**.

Raising children is the most difficult job in existence. Becoming a neurosurgeon or president or even an astronaut is easier than becoming a great parent. For all those jobs you can follow an educational plan or a manual.

To be a good parent, to not transfer any insecurities onto your child and to empower them to make their own choices, you have to put aside all your personal beliefs and values by solely focusing on your child's **I Am status**/toolbox of abilities and traits. It means adjusting your parenting style to what your child needs, each individual child in the family. It is a difficult task to raise a family without hang-ups and challenges.

This state of mind sees all is well even when life throws us a curve ball. This heaven, this utopia on earth can only be found inside you.

It centers on your personal toolbox, your attitude, recognition of your insecurities, responses, and your courage. We may know this and even claim that we do this, but if we did, that balance and peace would be reflected in the world at large. But if we start with ourselves, we have the opportunity to see miracles happen.

We need to empower others, not enable them by taking responsibilities that are not ours to carry.

Summary

- ✓ Everybody has this beautiful, magnificent inner light called our **I Am status**.
- ✓ This light gets buried during our lives under the teachings and expectations of others, the five-point system, family and societal cultures.
- ✓ Due to insecurities, we don't trust or can't find our **I Am status.**
- ✓ Our **I Am status** is the most valuable and useful thing we possess.
- ✓ Listening is an art, and there are three levels of listening.

- ✓ Level 1—internal listening: we are focused on ourselves.
- ✓ Level 2—focused listening: we are focused on the other.
- ✓ Level 3—global listening: we listen with all our senses.
- ✓ Miracles happen every day - we're blinded by our insecurities and false perceptions.
- ✓ Raising children without inflicting insecurities on them is nearly impossible.
- ✓ All the answers to the life questions you have will come from your **I Am status**.

CHAPTER 2

Trust

In the previous chapter we discovered the importance of our **I Am status**, what is the same as our toolbox, the influence of parents and the miracle of just being alive.

The first layer encountered in understanding human interaction is the impact of the five-point system on our behavior.

To help you visualize the five-point system, I've created some graphics. As we continue, layers will be added to the graph, making it easier to understand which layer is being discussed. In the next five chapters we will discuss each point individually.

What is Trust?

The definition of trust, according to the Canadian Oxford Dictionary, is "faith or confidence in the loyalty, veracity, reliability of a person or thing."

We often use the word trust, but how can we be sure that our definition of trust matches that of other people? Do we confuse it with honesty and truth? There are many questions with just as many answers.

Trust is not something you learn out of a schoolbook. We learn trust by experiencing life. The moment we are born we begin collecting data on trust. We build our definition of trust based on the feelings we experience at various times in our life.

For example, were your caregivers available when you needed them? Was there always enough food in the house? Did you feel safe?

If somebody asks you if you trust a person or thing, you will base your answer on past experiences.

Parents' Impact on Trust

If your parent/caregiver was always there for you and supported you, you will be less likely to have trust issues in relationships compared to somebody whose parents/caregivers weren't available.

Another form of trust is children trusting their parents and the school system to teach them what is true. Children naturally learn by example. Children copy their parent's way of speaking as well as their view of life.

The imprinting process is so subconscious that children are not even aware they are doing it. Children trusting what they see, hear and experience is normal. It is the way they learn to fit in.

For example, I adapted a twisted relationship with money that started with the how I saw my mother's relationship with money. For her spending money on something you didn't need was almost a sin. When something wasn't broken, like the bathroom or car, it was a shame to update or replace it.

This perspective of money's scarcity held me back for years until I started examining my connection to money. I found I had adopted my mother's perspective as my own truth.

I still feel this old thought pattern emerging at times. When I notice it, I refocus myself by asking, "Is this the truth that I think I know about money? What other perspectives are there? What else is possible?"

By refocusing I create an open space that gives me an opportunity to objectively look at where I want to go instead of staying on the path that does not serve me well or apply to my life.

What we think, we assume is the truth. Every thought in our heads we file as the truth. Often our thoughts are not even close to the truth.

Before examining my life, when I dealt with money, I consulted my experiences and found my mother's truth and circumstances.

She taught me that if something happened, she would be there for me. So how can the same person lie to me about how to deal with money? And if I don't follow my parents' view on money, does that mean I don't trust what they taught me? What does that say about me? Am I trustworthy?

These questions cross our minds so quickly we are not aware of them. These questions are subconsciously asked and answered before we reach the age of seven.

Many of our ideas regarding trust and truths are automatic. We barely notice from where they originate.

It changes when a new, sometimes-jarring, experience comes our way. This experience is added to our personal trust file, and when a new event occurs, we will draw it from our updated bank of memories.

Root Causes of Trust Issues

We naturally trust others. As babies, we have done so to survive. But in life we experience broken trust sometimes over and over again. This results in trust issues. The following are some root causes for trust issues:

- ✓ Social rejection
- ✓ Any form of abuse by a loved one
- ✓ Treatment as an outcast
- ✓ Being bullied
- ✓ Low self-esteem
- ✓ Loss of a loved one
- ✓ Post-traumatic stress
- ✓ Isolation

So what do we need to trust somebody or something?

To answer this question, I created a questionnaire based on using the five-point system with twelve multiple choice questions, which I sent to several people.
Its results reveal some of the factors individuals need to successfully feel all factors of the five-point system. If you'd like to take the questionnaire, it is included in Appendix C.

According to the question, to trust another person, most people felt the need to be able to be themselves, to be understood, to feel safe, and to feel heard.

Other factors mentioned were the absence of the threat of rejection, trusting their own sense of the person, spending time with a person to get to know them, knowing they are loyal, and seeing them do what they saw they will do.

Q12: What does it take for you to trust another person?

Need to feel safe	54.8%	23
Need to feel heard	40.5%	17
Need to feel understood	57.1%	24
That I can be myself	69.0%	29
Other	21.4%	9
		Answered question 42
		Skipped question 1

(Survey conducted courtesy of SurveyMonkey Inc.)[1]

"Other" responses:

1. All the above, especially that I "can be myself" without heightened sense of being rejected.

---

[1] SurveyMonkey Inc., Palo Alto, California, USA, accessed November 15, 2012, www.surveymonkey.com.

Mostly, to trust another, I need to trust myself and my own discernment of another's honesty and trustworthiness.
2. All of the above.
3. Good to get to know them and spend time with them.
4. Learned through experience that I can trust the other person.
5. I need to know them well enough to really trust. However, I will normally trust people until they do something to change my attitude.
6. They say what they mean and do what they are going to do.
7. All of the above.
8. True trust is rare for me. Need to know person is loyal.
9. Need to know person is loyal

When we say, "I trust," we are expressing a feeling and not stating a fact. We believe trust is a fact, and by doing so we create confusion within ourselves that will result in doubting our own inner wisdom.

Believing trust is a fact, not a feeling, puts us out of touch with our **I Am status** and leads to trust issues with ourselves and others.

Truth/Honesty

To see the difference, we need to look at the two main ingredients of trust: honesty and truth.

> Truth: the quality or a state of being true, conformity to fact or reality
> Honesty: the quality of being honest, fair in character or behavior

What's the difference between truth and honesty?

Truth is more tangible and measurable.

Honesty is based on a personal, emotional point of view. We can be honest, but that doesn't mean what we feel is true.

Here are some examples of the difference between truth and honesty.

Honesty	Truth
I feel shame and guilt that I spent so much money on clothes today.	I spent $65 for a blouse, $125 on pants, and $60 for shoes. That was $125, over the budget I set for myself today.
I want to lose weight.	I eat more in a day than what my body needs.

This bill was too high. I don't think I need to pay all that.	I didn't pay the whole bill.
I want to take motorcycle lessons.	I haven't scheduled a training session.

The difference isn't always easy to see. There are many grey areas.

Consider my view on money. My mother taught me about money and how to make the best of it, from her honest point of view. She did a great job and gave me useful tips and strategies to make the most of money it were scarce. But is that the truth?

In her life experience, to pay the bills she really needed to watch the money and make choices on what was important to her. She never knew when the next disaster would hit, and therefore she needed to save for a rainy day. That situation was her truth and reality.

But it is not automatically the truth for everybody?

I thought it was a universal truth for the longest time because it was what I saw, experienced, tasted, and heard from the time I was born. My opinion changed when I really started asking, what is my truth, my reality?

I found my personal truth different from my mother's experience and I shifted from her scarcity perspective to my view of my money situation. I still pay attention to how I spend my money and have a good handle on my finances without the blame and shame I once adopted.

Is this the truth for everybody? Maybe, maybe not. You have to find out what is true for yourself. For some people, it doesn't matter how much money they have, it still isn't enough whether you live paycheque to paycheque or have millions in the bank. We choose our personal mindset but not always consciously.

How to Find Your Truth

It only becomes a truthful answer when you examine all the thoughts that lead up to the conclusion. The moment you start to dissect your conscious thoughts, the more your subconscious thoughts come to the front. It will look like a bottomless pit with many side tunnels.

What you create is a spider web with truth in the middle and questions on the outside. The truth is not always that easy to see, not even inside ourselves.

The flip side is when you find your truth, it is very hard to ignore it or go back to old ways. Your **I Am status** won't let you. If you do ignore the truth, you know you are betraying yourself, which is the highest form of betrayal. You can't hide behind your beliefs anymore, you will seek the truth because by living your truth your life has less drama and feels lighter, though not necessarily, easier.

When seeking the truth, you will encounter your insecurities, and they will put up a fight if you try to change or banish them.

Hidden Truths

Sometimes there are truths we can't see directly. They may be out of our vision field or hidden. Truths out of our vision field are those things we have no experience or knowledge about so we have to trust that the information we are given by others is correct.

For example, biologists report that wild tiger numbers are at a record low, and tigers are on the endangered species list. The measurable numbers are low, so we believe it to be a truth, though we have no interaction with tigers. We don't have enough experience or evidence because it is out of our vision field. So we trust the information and make decisions based on that knowledge.

Hidden truths are tricky because they are not always clearly a truth, an opinion or another person's situation. Every conversation you have with others can contain a truth or fact, depending on the situation and source of information.

Fact or Truth

For example, what we teach children varies. We teach them how to add, which is a concrete fact and truth. We also teach them according to our situation. If the economy is poor and finances limited, we teach them to conserve money.

It is important to be as honest with yourself as you can, brutally honest. The more honest you are with yourself, the more in touch you are with your **I Am status**, which will lead you to see the truth more easily. In turn, this will boost your self-esteem and help you make solid decisions during the challenges in life.

Personal Exercise:
Start by asking yourself, do I trust myself?

Test your trust in yourself by asking simple questions and listening for inner answers. Ask yourself, "What do you want to eat?"

Will your answer be, "I don't know."

You do know what you want to eat. But you also know what you want isn't always good for you. The answer may be a hamburger or chocolate bar, sometimes it will be salad.

Asking such questions is a way of checking-in with yourself and learning to trust that although you may know what you want, you also know what is best for you.

This check-in method can be used for most situations in your life. The obstacle to overcome is being honest with ourselves and not looking for answers to please somebody else.

Ask yourself this, "If I can't be honest and truthful with myself, how can I be honest and truthful with others?" The circle in life always starts with us, nobody else.

Denying Your Inner Truth & Its Effects

If you deny your inner truth, you deny truth. You create a fantasy world and try to live there, not in reality. When we waver between fantasy and reality, we have difficulty trusting what we see, feel, touch, smell, and hear.

The circle of life based on fantasy makes us afraid, untrusting, skeptical, cynical and miserable.

Today's world seems to be wavering between fantasy and reality. When more people trust themselves and teach their children to trust their inner guides, we can tip the scale to reality and deal with all we face, without fear's paralyzing grip. Sometimes, being true to oneself leads to going against family traditions.

Family and Truth

We've all experienced a family member who didn't follow family/cultural traditions or whose choices were out of the ordinary. That family member may receive looks of disapproval or judgment or may feel unworthy, feel like an outcast. Often families talk about those family members for years and not always in an understanding way.

These creations of shame, blame, and guilt for those who choose to follow their own path make parents protective of their children and themselves. Afraid of losing their own social status they forget to focus on their inner wisdom or allow the expectations of others to dictate their reactions.

Family Influences

To uncover family reactions, I surveyed people, asking them, "What is the effect on you when you decide to go against your family/friends wishes?"

Most noted that they take their family and friends' concerns into consideration but, in the end, trust their gut feelings. For some, it made them insecure and hesitant to proceed and for others it shut them down and made them forget all about their dreams. Some responded that it was a combination of all three effects, depending on the situation.

The results show that most of the time, we pay attention to what we know is best for us.

Q5: What is the effect on you when you decide to go against your family/friends wishes?

I shut down and forget all about my dreams	4.8%	2
I feel insecure and hesitate to proceed	19.0%	8
I take my family and friends concerns into consideration but will (in the end) trust my own gut feeling	73.8%	31
other	9.5%	4
		Answered question 42
		Skipped question 1

(Survey conducted courtesy of SurveyMonkey Inc.)[2]

"Other" responses.

1. I also realize that family and friends have contributed to my gut feeling as often people share their advise and I needed to hear it. This has given me ample opportunities to make wiser decisions.
2. Sometimes #1, sometimes #2 and occaissionally#3
3. Emphasis on "in the end".
4. My first chakra goes nuts.

---

[2] Ibid.

I' glad to see that 73.8% of the participants trust their inner wisdom.

What is trust, and what does it look like? The answer is not that simple, because trust is a feeling and is different for everyone. The best I can do is describing my own feelings of trust.

When I trust a person or a situation, I feeling relaxed and safe, and I can let down my guard. I don't have to present myself as better than I am. I don't have to play games. I don't feel judged or attacked. What you see is what you get.

Many people have a hard time trusting their inner wisdom. For some it takes years to learn to listen and trust themselves. They ask for advice on everything from everybody—from clothes to wear to what type of car to drive, how to behave in certain situations, even how to celebrate occasions like weddings, holidays and birthdays. People can't get past feeling guilty or ashamed doing what they want to do instead of what they advised or told to do.

Body Language

We learn to camouflage our true feelings, hiding behind a wall of politeness. It is hard to see from the outside what happens on the inside. However, if you look closely, you will see through facial expressions, tones of voice and body language a person's true state of mind. People talk more with their body than with words.

It is one thing for you to trust somebody. It's another for them to find you trustworthy. How can you tell if somebody finds you trustworthy?

The biggest compliment a person can give you is to be vulnerable with you. People sharing their thoughts and feelings in a way that shows what an impact situations have had on them is a priceless gift and treated with respect.

That is trust at the highest level. That doesn't mean you have to agree with what is being said. It only means that you listen to somebody else's point of view and that you respect that view, even when your view is different.

That's why trust is so fragile and so quickly broken. We often listen at Level 1 to what someone is saying, and don't pay enough attention to their words and how they are saying it with their body language and tone of voice.

Three Layers of Trust

To avoid quickly judging people, we need to practice forgiveness and gratitude.

The quickest way not to judge would be to always do what you said you would do, no shortcuts or excuses.

However, life happens. That's why gratitude and forgiveness are essential tools for a great and prosperous life.

It is healthier not to trust blindly but to ask more life questions. Let's take a look at all the levels of trust we encounter and the life questions we can ask.

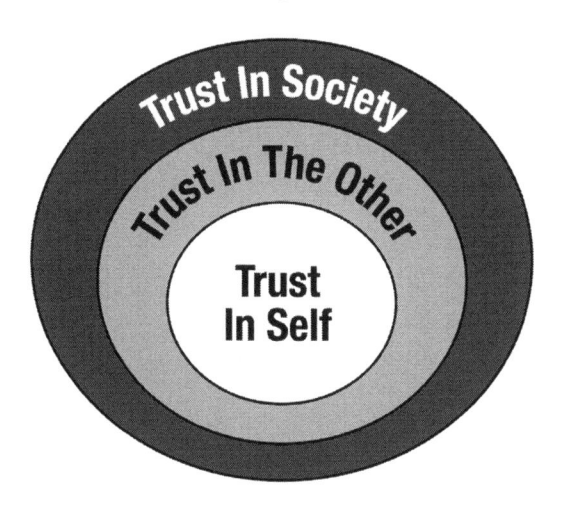

Trust In Society / Trust In The Other / Trust In Self

First Layer - Trust in Self

Let's start with the first layer - trust in self. This is complicated, especially when you have trust issues created by others (see the trust issues column). When you have difficulty trusting others, you also will have issues trusting yourself. This shows in the imprint theory.

If you haven't experienced trust trauma created by others, can you experience trust issues? In our lives others will disappoint us at one point or another. What makes the difference is how deep the disappointment runs. We all have scratches, but some are deeper than others. Some you can repair, some are almost impossible to fix.

Learn From Past Disappointments

When disappointed you believe you are the victim of what is done to you, and it affects your outlook and ability to trust. But ask yourself - how often in the last two weeks have I disappointed someone or broken a promise?

By telling this truth to yourself, you will see that you've scratched somebody else's trust in the way others have done to you.

We often see ourselves as victims, but just as often we are the attackers. To see and acknowledge that statement is the first step to personal healing. When we are truthful toward ourselves, we can start making conscious choices to be graceful and forgiving in the quest to start healing our scratches.

Difference Between Confidence and Arrogance

If you have strong self-esteem and are happy with yourself, subconsciously or maybe even consciously, you will make decisions with your inner wisdom. This allows you to be confident, which others sometimes view as being arrogant. You may, at times, view those with self-confidence as arrogant.

The difference lays in the intention, the energy, and the attitude in which something is done or presented.

When you are arrogant, your intention is often to gain materially by your actions, your energy is heavy and demanding, and your attitude is that the world owes you what you selfishly want.

When you are confident, your intention is to create happiness in life, the energy is light and warm, and your attitude is open and willing to share with others.

Don't assume you are one or the other. People generally fluctuate between confidence and arrogance, depending on the day and situation.

In daily life, we are often not aware of our personal intentions, energy, and attitudes, let alone how we come across to others.

Taking personal responsibility for your actions will help you in every relationship you will ever be in. Being a partner, a coworker, a friend, a committee member and a family member means demonstrating trustworthiness by paying attention to what you say (not gossiping or verbally hurting others) and taking responsibility for all your actions. When you make an error, keep in mind that a sincere apology is often the only answer. The question here is not if you make a misstep but when you make one, how do you respond.

The sooner we realize that everybody slips up once in a while, the quicker we have compassion for ourselves and others when mistakes are made.

Embrace Mistakes, Fight the Fear

Most of us are so afraid of failure and mistakes that our fear cripples us. I have seen it in the people around me, and in myself. Depending on the group around me, I can be afraid to do new things and try something out of the ordinary.

I've seen fearful moments last too long, some of them years. Some of those fears cost people money, friendships and unproductive time.

Fearful moments will come into your life. Each contains a lesson or skill you may need at a later date.

The moment you start trusting yourself, the easier it is to trust others. It is a necessary step to learning more about what makes people do the things they do.

When miscommunication occurs, try to place yourself in another's shoes to discover their viewpoint. This makes it easier to forgive and have compassion for all involved, including yourself.

Make friends with failure, and see it as a tool to move through your own personal mud. When you take the opportunity to learn, not shut down, you often emerge a better person with a new skill set.

How will you know that you've experienced success if you've never failed? Failure is an instrument to help us stretch ourselves beyond what is comfortable.

Second Layer - Trust in Others

To measure our trustworthiness we have to look at the second layer, trust in others. Our trustworthiness shows in the second or third layer because it is difficult to be objective toward ourselves. We can't see ourselves the way others see us.

Trust in others is more challenging because we are dealing with another human being and their thoughts, insecurities, and wishes. Depending on their communication skills, those thoughts and wishes may come across poorly. Assumptions by both parties, create confusion which can result in blame and/or shame feelings in one or both parties.

Showing Trust When Parenting

Just look at trust between parents and their children. Parents do their best to teach their children trust. The sticking point comes when they show trust in them. Parents want to protect their children from making mistakes. If they do this by being controlling about everything, it communicates that the parent does not trust them to make decisions, no matter how much they say they do. Actions speak the loudest. As a result, kids may believe themselves untrustworthy.

Parents need to know when to trust that they've taught their children to make the right decisions. This is easier if they begin when the children are young by giving their children the opportunity to make small decisions first. Starting by letting them go around the block by themselves when they are seven or so, and expanding to letting them go to the park for an hour with older friends when they are eight.

Of course, it all depends where you live and what the situation is, but by letting children take on responsibility that they can handle, parents demonstrate with actions, not just words, that they trust their children's judgment.

Children will gain more trust in themselves. These days, with all the fear and negative media, we often step in too soon. Overprotected children may not trust their inner wisdom because Mom and Dad have always done their fighting for them. This is simple to say but difficult to do. Having raised three sons, I understand the fine balance between trust and safety.

Recognizing Our Mistakes

To begin to forgive ourselves, we first have to admit we've made a mistake. This is the next best thing we can do for ourselves. It is also an important lesson to teach our children. Despite how good our intentions are, we never know what is best for other people.

As a mother, I understand how hard this is to do with ourselves and with our children. My sons are in their twenties, and it is still hard to let them make their own choices and mistakes. I have to trust that I've taught them the life skills they need to live their own lives.

Have you ever admitted a mistake to your child?

My dad did, and I still feel the impact today. I had to be home at 12:30 p.m. for dinner, and I got home at exactly 12.30 p.m. My family, however, was already eating. My dad got mad, and he hit me for being late. When my mom said that I was on time and that they had started eating early, he apologized. It was so powerful when he said he was sorry and that he was wrong, that now almost forty years later I still remember the warm, fuzzy understanding feeling I got after his apology.

I still use this as an example in my own life. When I make a mistake, I will own up to it and try to make it right by not letting pride get in the way. Admitting you were wrong shows you are human. Admitting you've made a mistake shows your children that parents can make mistakes too. You also show that making mistakes in itself is not bad. What counts is how you take the responsibility to make things right.

By doing owning up to your mistakes, parents show their children the power of personal responsibility and teaches, through example, that kids can own their responsibilities.

Third Layer - Trust in Society

The third layer of trust is more complicated - trust in society. When you look around and watch the news, you may ask yourself, "Who can I trust?" The government? The health-care system? The education system? The justice system? The banks?

It is overwhelming, like standing at the foot of a mountain and not knowing what it is. Figuring out who to trust and where to start is not an easy task. This mountain is so high you can't see over or around it. The only way is to climb it is one step at a time.

Is everything they say in the news true? I would hope so. I assume they've done their homework and only report the facts. But that is not always true, even when the people involved do their absolute best to remain neutral. Mistakes are made. Facts missed. Issues simplified.

In her book, <u>Anatomy of the Spirit</u>, Caroline Myss described a building on fire with four reporters on each corner. The result is that you will likely get four different stories about what happened at the fire. Each reporter has their own perspective of the event. Even when you are trained, as reporters are, to keep emotions out of a story, your personality and perspective will seep into the writing. If that was not the case, then everybody would be the same, and the world would be a monotonous place with no personality.

For people, writing and talking about how they perceive the world is a great place to start communicating. As I share my point of view with you, I trust in myself that what I write is true. I leave it up to you to form your own opinion and apply what you read to your life experience.

We all know when we look deep inside what we can trust and what we can't. We get so blinded by what other people tell us that we start questioning ourselves.

The news might take a story and make it big and dramatic because the more dramatic the story, the more papers are sold and the more money made. It is a sad but true truth. Newspapers are not non-profits. If there was no pressure to make a profit in news reporting and broadcasting, the news would look very different. Sometimes the more coverage a news event gets, the more similar events are picked up. For example, a highly publicized shooting often results in greater coverage of shootings of any nature.

As I've started to look objectively at advertising and commercials I've come to the conclusion that if you believe less than half of what they promise you, you'll be in the right ballpark. Commercials are like novels good to escape with, full of drama but very little substance. There may be a kernel of truth in the story but not much more.

To make it more confusing, we have the Internet spreading news worldwide in seconds. As our global society hears of events from across the world, we all feel the emotional impact of the story. Since most news is negative, it affects our view of our life, our country and our world. Due the vastness of the world and the variety of governments, cultures and practices, we are faced with more hidden truths.

For example, when we compare vegetables by price, it appears some locally grown vegetables are more expensive than imported produce. What we don't know is that due to stricter pesticide and insecticide regulation, the cost of labor and equipment, locally produced vegetables may be safer to consume. In a global society, we often assume that food or products are handled the same way as our home country but differences in cleanliness standards, workplace safety, wages, cost of living and production standards create hidden truths that challenge our already fragile trust in a world society.

Populations all over the world are losing trust in their governments. The increased reports of protests, grassroots disengagement and acts of violence by governments against their own citizens makes one wonder, can we change and create trust in society? It is not impossible, but it will take a lot of work and excellent communication skills from everybody. We have to keep in mind that a century ago a person's society was their family and the local village.

When radio, then TV was introduced, a person's personal experience of society expanded to include nations.

These days we can travel the world in twenty-six hours, with the Internet providing instant information.

The trick for us is to build time into our day. Stopping and reflecting continuously about what is important for us right here, right now, without getting swept away in the whirlwind of information that, if given a chance, can begin to rule our lives.

These days all transactions - money, food, products, services, health care and education are so complex the average person does not understand or know all the details. Everything is so specialized that we lose contact with the whole picture. What results are chaos, envy, and unworthiness, which makes it a challenge to have trust in our global society.

Summary

- ✓ Trust is an emotion, not a fact.
- ✓ Trust has two main components: honesty and truth.
- ✓ Honesty comes from a personal, emotional point of view.
- ✓ Truth is measurable - it is or is not.
- ✓ Parents/caregivers are the first ones to teach about trust.
- ✓ Trust issues are often created based on how others treated us when we were young or by major events later in life.
- ✓ Trusting yourself starts by being honest with yourself.
- ✓ Being trustworthy starts with doing what you say you will do, matching your words with your actions.
- ✓ There are three layers of trust:
- ✓ Trust in self is what everything starts with. Self-esteem is the foundation for the way you view life.
- ✓ Trust in others is more complicated. Now you not only deal with your own trust insecurities but also with those of others.
- ✓ Trust in society is challenged by the clouded ways and hidden truths of how the world works these days.

CHAPTER 3

Conflict

The one thing all relationships have, at some point, is conflict. Conflict inspires so many questions - What is the cause of this conflict? Why are we going in circles? Will we ever solve this issue? How can we solve it? Why can't they understand my point of view? What don't they understand?

You may think that if the other person would just look farther than their nose is long, this conflict would not be happening.

The cause of almost all conflicts stems from the following issues:

- ✓ Personal stress
- ✓ Taking everything personally
- ✓ Being judgmental
- ✓ Making assumptions

- ✓ Betraying yourself and/or others
- ✓ Not taking personal responsibility
- ✓ Being unfamiliar with a new family or societal culture
- ✓ Not trusting yourself or another
- ✓ Misinterpreting communication

As you can see, the root of almost every conflict has nothing to do with the event that triggers it. Often conflict is a combination of the above elements all at once. However, most of us are not even aware that this is the case. We are so caught up in everyday events or the fight that we can't pinpoint the root cause. We only focus on the fight itself. By doing so, we don't see the solution to the real problem. Problems magnify and get blown out of proportions. By not settling the issue, problems fester and more conflicts happen.

We all have different patterns we use when dealing with a conflict:

- ✓ Avoiding issues
- ✓ Dismissing the issues
- ✓ Closing oneself off or becoming a brick wall
- ✓ Acting like a martyr or victim
- ✓ Attacking and being confrontational

Between the causes and the coping strategies we use, it is no wonder that we keep creating drama and arguments.

If our goal is to live a life filled with harmony and inner peace, we have to start recognizing, focusing on and improving the coping strategies we use when in conflict.

Conflict Is Positive?

We need to take personal responsibility for what we want out of life. Expanding our understanding of conflict itself will help us refocus our intention. For most of us the word conflict has a negative connotation.

What would happen if we viewed every argument as a tool to expand our personal view and broaden our comfort zone?

Conflict then becomes healthy and can make you grow mentally and emotionally as a human being. Life constantly provides us with opportunities to grow and expand. We make the decisions about what we do with these chances.

Causes of conflict intertwine. Betraying yourself will trigger you to take everything personally, creating more personal stress. When you make assumptions and judgments, you are not taking responsibility for your actions. At this point, clear communication is not possible, and arguments become inevitable.

Working with a conflict is no different than opening yourself up to your truths and inner wisdom. Don't betray yourself by automatically assuming the role of victim in a conflict. Go back to your core, you're **I Am status**. Draw from this inner strength what you need to have a clear head when engaging in an argument and come up with a good solution for everyone.

Trust is the core when dealing with any part of the five-part system. It keeps you in touch with your **I Am status**.

Managing Stress

Personal stress is an umbrella term for daily living. Every day is filled with moments that challenge our stress meter. Sometimes it is work, home, family, friends, or media. It can all of the above at some point in our day. How we deal with stress depends on how we feel at that moment.

If we are happy and relaxed, we will react differently to the same event than when we are already stressed. For example, let's say that your stress meter is triggered before you leave home because the children woke up grumpy and didn't want to cooperate in getting ready for school, which means you're running late. The chances are that when something else happens, say the elevator is broken and you have to walk up six flights of stairs, you won't be a happy camper by the time you are behind your desk.

All this happens before 9:00 a.m. and you haven't even dealt with your boss yet. It will be more difficult to deal with another setback than if you had an easy morning with everything running like clockwork.

Stress often builds up over time. The first thing is fine; the second setback is challenging; the third setback is frustrating, and by time the fourth problem occurs, you explode. As stress increases we put up walls as a coping mechanism. The moment those are in place it is almost impossible to see and be open to a different point of view.

Walls reduce our listening to a Level 1 automatically, which will increase the chances of miscommunication and create fuel for festering frustration. This potential time bomb may explode later with little provocation. Nothing gets resolved, and this cycle can repeat itself for a long time, decades even.

Conflict Coping Mechanisms

A person I know acts the martyr or victim as their conflict coping mechanisms, followed by being confrontational. Their spouse dismisses the issues and closes them self off. When they are in conflict, the spouse gets very quiet and won't say a word. This might go on for hours, even days. This behavior drives the other person crazy, and they begin to nag, even scream to get the other person to talk. My friend judges their spouse as being unyielding and childish.

After one such fight, something changed. They fought in the usual way, one being mad and one being quiet. The next day, my friend talked to a therapist about the fight. The therapist asked her how long this pattern had been going on. My friend replied, "At least twenty years." She was hoping to get some sympathy from therapist and thought the therapist would be on her side. Instead she said, "When something like this happens, your spouse knows (or assumes) how you will react, the same as you know how he will react because that has been the pattern for the last twenty years. To change his reaction you have to change yours first because you are aware of the circle you are in."

Sure enough, a couple of months later something happened that triggered a fight and my friend's spouse went quiet. She remembered her talk with the therapist, and did something different. Instead of going on the defensive, she ignored him. If she had a question, she asked it politely. He didn't know what was going on. By changing her behavior, she changed the way they dealt with conflict.

When we are in conflict with someone, we have to try different strategies before we find a strategy that works. As a result, there will likely be more than one conflict. Each person has their own range of coping mechanisms we need to be able to identify.

To become better at engaging in conflict we need first, to be aware of our personal coping mechanisms.

Once you've figured out your own conflict pattern, stop and experiment with how to deal with conflict in a different manner. This works with kids fighting against doing homework as well as it does with workplace disagreements and personality clashes.

When I surveyed people and asked the question, "How do you react when conflict arises?" most people answered that they try to stay calm and not take it personally, while others said they act defensively. The third most popular answer was that they turn inward and refuse to speak to the other person, sometimes for hours or even days, followed by those who pretend nothing is happening and hope it blows over. The answer, "I immediately launch into a counterattack" was favored by only one person out of 43 surveyed.

Q2: How do you react when conflict arises?

I act defensively.	34.9%	15
I pretend nothing is happening and hope it blows over.	7.9%	3
I turn inward and refuse to speak to the other person, sometimes for hours or even days.	11.6%	5

I try to stay calm and not take it personal.	62.8%	27
I immediately launch into a counterattack.	2.3%	1
Other	23.3%	10
		Answered question 43
		Skipped question 0

(Survey conducted courtesy of SurveyMonkey Inc.)[3]

"Other" responses:

1. All of the above, depending ... Then, I slow it down, and honor all my feelings about it, and then I choose how I want to respond.
2. I believe conflict is healthy. It is useful for expressing opinions, and for working through things. I have no issue with conflict. I welcome it. I often will purposefully enter the "area of danger" for the purpose of strengthening understanding. Bringing clarity and solidifying the relationship.
3. That is how I like to think I react but also feel a blow inside me and quietly I am defensive.
4. I try not act defensively, and try to really listen to the problem behind the problem. Sometimes it is hard; to keep my emotions in check if I feel

---

[3] Ibid.

not "seen." I try to remember it is about the other person and not a comment about me.
5. I try to think about it, wait at least a few hours and then face the issue.
6. It depends on the situation and the person; I don't have one dominant response to conflict.
7. Tears (usually inwards) may come but I go over things myself to determine if I may have been some part of the cause of the conflict. If I am, I try to make amends with an apology.
8. Depends on the day, time, how I'm feeling and just what the conflict is … … … I'd like to say I stay calm and not take it personal, but I suspect that more often than not I either act defensively of counter attack.
9. Emphasis on the word "try."
10. Take a leadership role.

It is great to see that 62.8% try to stay calm and not take it personally. When you read the "Other" responses, you get a closer look at how people cope differently with conflict. I didn't edit the responses I got, because I wanted the responses to be real and honest. Based on this survey, most us try to stay calm and not take everything personally.

Taking Things Personally

So why do we have so much conflict in our relationships? And why is it so difficult to stay calm and not take everything personally? Taking everything personally is the next root cause of conflict.

I wondered if there was a correlation between emotional connection and the difficulty of conflict, so I asked those I survey, "Does your reaction to conflict change within different relationships, say parents/partner or strangers?"

The response was an overwhelming yes. When asked how it was different, I came to the conclusion that for most people, the closer you are to somebody, the more difficult it gets to not take everything personally and to stay calm.

Q3: Does your reaction to conflict change within different relationships, say parents/partner or strangers?

Yes	29.3%	12
No	14.6%	6
If yes, how?	56.1%	23
		Answered Questions 41
		Skipped question 0

(Survey conducted courtesy of SurveyMonkey Inc.)[4]

---

[4] Ibid.

"Other" responses:

1. My relationships are with different characters therefore conflict resolution take on slightly different aspects. Conflict with my twin sister is rare and intuitively resolved. Conflict with the other members of my family requires much more communication.
2. With my friends I don't react as, let's call it intense as with my family.
3. I stay with people I care about and with whom I want to continue a relationship.
4. Tend to hold off on the immediate and think through the consequences.
5. The closer the relationship, the more conflict will hurt it seems.
6. Depends on how well I know the person. At times if I know them well, I might just hope
7. it blows over.
8. The closer the person is to me, the more it hurts me. On the other hand I try to resolve the conflict always the same way.
9. I react differently with people I am close to as I feel that they will understand my venting. Strangers would never know I was upset or angry. If someone is close to you it hurts more.
10. React faster if it is family.

11. Handling conflicts with relatives may be more difficult as there is a more emotional aspect involved.
12. With my mother, I tend to avoid and not talk about it, wait for it to blow over. Partner, I tend to get defensive. Strangers or clients, I try to stay calm and professional, ask questions and find a solution.
13. Not sure, but I don't feel the pressure on my chest sometimes.
14. In some relationships it is easier to talk about conflict right away because of how the other person reacts/deals with conflict. If however someone else shuts down and won't communicate then I tend to do the same. After many years of trying to discuss and the other person won't, you just learn to do the same.
15. With people I deal with everyday, (and closer to me) it is more necessary to forgive and forget but harder to do than with a stranger.
16. It may depend on the history of the relationship.
17. With some you can stand up for what you believe, but say parents I try and lay low and wait for things to blow over, never really resolving things.
18. I may not think too long if it is parents/partner.

19. I have different reactions to different people. With some people I feel defensive, with others I can completely not take things personally.
20. The closer the relationship I have with someone, the more I react. It's easy to walk away from a stranger as you might never have occasion to see them again.
21. The closer the relationship the more potentially disturbing the conflict.
22. I take family conflict more personally, and I find them much harder on the heart than when dealing with friends or associates.
23. With close relationships it is harder not to take things personal.

Role of Trust in Healthy Conflict

Emotions play a big role for most people when in conflict. We all know that, but what about trust? Is there a connection between feeling safe and significant in a relationship and healthy conflict? I believe there is.

When you feel safe and important to another person in a conflict, you trust that the other person still has your best interests in mind and is not there to hurt you.

When my father in-law and I were in conflict, whether it was about the farm or a personal matter, I could tell him to take a hike. Similarly, he could tell me, "Ellen, it is enough," and I would know that was that was as far as I could go. But we always came back later to discuss the problem and always resolved our conflicts.

This, of course, is a two-way street. Both people in the conflict have to be willing to step back and cool off before talking about it again. This cool-off period doesn't have to take days or weeks, sometimes it just takes an hour. However, the main thing is not to "forget" to revisit the issue because, even if it feels easier, if you don't talk about the issue, it will fester and unresolved feelings will build up. That leads to assumptions, judgment and ends in blaming the other person for the conflict, and the downward spiral into conflict begins again.

When you are at this point, it is harder to clear the air, and you will likely end up going in circles. Nobody wins in this situation, but everybody loses. Sometimes we are so afraid of hurting the ones we love and losing their trust that we think by playing down issues and not being upfront with our frustrations we will save a strained relationship. In fact, it makes the relationship worse and draws the conflict out longer, because no one moves to resolve it.

The survey answers seem to indicate that the less emotionally attached you are to the person you have a conflict with, the easier it is to detach yourself and the more clearheaded you can be when you enter the confrontational zone. This is because they don't have power over your emotions and self-worth.

This is where personal responsibly is important. We can't expect somebody else to be solely responsible for our well-being. It is our personal responsibility to be in charge of our lives. This sounds so simple and full of common sense.

So why do we blame others when something doesn't go according to plan and conflict arises?

We are reluctant to step up and declare our needs—not our wants but the needs that have to be in place so that we don't betray ourselves. Don't confuse this with material well-being, like housing or the car you drive.

I'm talking about situations that threaten your core values, the center of your being from which you make all the important decisions in life.

Making Assumptions

A big cause of conflict is assumptions. We as a human race assume on almost a daily basis. Sometimes our assumptions are true, but most times they are not. If you think you know what other people want or think, nine out of ten times you will be wrong.

Conflict and assumptions often go hand in hand. When we are in conflict with ourselves, we take it out on the people around us. To get to the core of the battle, ask yourself - Is the real conflict about me, the event, or the other person? If we don't ask that question, we open ourselves to confusion. In the survey, I asked "How often do you assume that you know what other people think and do (particularly close family and friends)?"

Most people answered that they sometimes assume (47.6%), followed by the answer, "I assume more times than I realize" (42.9%). Fewer people answered "I realize that I'm always assuming till somebody tells what they think and feel" (16.7%) while the least popular responses were "I do not realize that I'm assuming" (4.8%) and I never assume because I know my people (2.4%).

Q9: How often do you assume that you know what other people think and do (particularly close family and friends)?

I never assume because I know my people.	2.4%	1
I sometimes assume.	47.6%	20
I assume more times then I realize.	42.9%	18
I realize that I'm always assuming till somebody tells me what they think and feel.	16.7%	7

I do not realize that I'm assuming.	4.8%	2
Other	9.5%	4
		Answered question 42
		Skipped question 1

(Survey conducted courtesy of SurveyMonkey Inc.)[5]

"Other" responses:

1. People tell me what they think and feel directly and indirectly. Mostly, I listen to what they say, and the actions that they make, to try to understand what is happening and why.
2. I try not to assume. I like to ask them.
3. That's a tough one. I try to be sensitive to their feelings. If I'm not sure and don't feel it's appropriate to ask, a hug can sometimes do the trick.
4. A combination.

While a majority of questionnaire participants are aware that they assume at times, it is accurate to say that we always will assume to a certain degree. Assumptions are even necessary.

---

[5] Ibid.

When we look outside in the morning, we guess the temperature and dress accordingly. We assume we will wake up every morning.

There are times when making assumptions is appropriate.

It is the other times when we assume which causes conflict and misunderstandings. When young children ask a million seemingly random questions, I smile. They are so curious about the world around them and want to know everything. What they don't do is assume they know the answer to the questions.

Around age seven, children gradually stop asking as many questions. As children age, we expect them to be more "grown up." They begin to use reason, logic, knowledge and assumptions to find the answers.

Asking Powerful Questions

Why are assumptions dangerous for relationships? If you answer a question yourself about somebody else's, instead of asking the person who can give you a clear answer, you could get in trouble with the conclusion you make.

What if you are guessing which chemicals you can mix together instead of knowing how each chemical reacts with the others?

You may have a bomb on your hands.

That is what happens every time you guess someone's response to a question, instead of asking for their response.

You can sidestep such a minefield if you ask many powerful questions in almost every conversation you have. Use different types of questions to learn more about a person.

The following types of questions tend to create strained and defensive conversations:

Leading questions that give us the answers we want to hear.

Questions put the other person on the defensive and sound like we are judging the answers we receive.

Questions beginning with "Why did you …?" or "Do you …?"

Questions that strain dialogue and resurrect old patters and belief systems that lead to more conflict.

Using these types of questions to collect information puts the other person on the defensive.

A powerful question is one born out of curiosity and exploration. Seeking the other person's point of view leads to learning and conveys a sincere interest in them. Because you are curious and not attached to the outcome, you leave your assumptions and judgments out of the conversation, and nobody sits in the witness chair or goes on the defensive.

Conversations that are open and nonjudgmental revolve around powerful questions that make a person stop and think. These questions create a response, not a reaction

Powerful questions begin with:
What ....?
When .....?
How ....?

- ✓ Instead of asking - "Why didn't you e-mail me about the changes in the meeting date?" (defensive?=reaction),
- ✓ ask "What happened that you forgot to e-mail me about the changes in the meeting date?" (curious?=response)

Ask powerful questions. It works to diffuse most situations and keep the lines of communication open. Few people like to be told what to do and when. By being curious, we give up our attachment to a certain outcome.

Family & Societal Culture

This flows into the next cause of conflict: family and/or societal culture.

It is disorienting when you move into a new family and have to learn how to interact within a different family structure than the one you grew up with.

Every family has its own set of norms, regulations and belief systems. You could say each family has its own culture inside the larger societal culture. When a new member comes in with different experiences and beliefs, there's bound to be some friction. All of a sudden these new family members are questioning your norms and regulations just as much as you are questioning theirs.

Most people go into defensive mode when our way of living is questioned by others. We question or judge the new viewpoints and, most of the time, reject them because we think that if we accept the new point of view, we have to trade in our own belief system.

People know what they know, and adapting to change is difficult.

Being Judgmental

Another big element of conflict is being judgmental. It is as damaging, if not more, than making assumptions. We often fail to see the damage judgment does. Most of the time, we are not even aware that we are judging ourselves and others.

There is a difference between making a judgment and stating an observation or point of view. The biggest difference lies in what you say and how you say it.

If a forty year old, overweight lady with orange hair, dressed in a pink, flowery dress, wearing red high heels, a red purse, and blue hat is walking down the street, internally you may judge her by thinking, "Look at that fat, ugly lady. She doesn't have any taste and shouldn't be allowed to dress herself. I don't think she is totally there, if you know what I mean!"

Stating your point of view on the same lady, would be saying, "What that lady is wearing is not flattering on her. It doesn't enhance her figure, in my opinion."

When discussing youth who steal cars and commit violence, it is so easy to judge them, dismissing them as good-for-nothing trash that deserve to be locked up and punished. When we judge we see the youth as objects, not as people with stories and feelings.

Someone stating their point of view on the same youths might say, "I'm not okay with the stealing and the violence. There should be repercussions for those actions, but I wonder what kind of life those kids have that they see violence as the only way out. What change is needed in society so that we can break the cycle these kids are stuck in?"

When you communicate with a person who is in a judgmental state of mind, there is no way to negotiate your thoughts or point of view. The person has already made up their mind about how you or something should be and are rarely open to new ideas. It is hard to change somebody's thinking patterns, when they are being judgmental.

When you are in a conversation with judgment, you feel as if you are talking to a brick wall without a door and with no way around it. The only thing you can do is bang your head against it.

Or is it?

What would happen if you let go of your judgments and assumptions?

Due to my perspective and personal experiences I choose to be open-minded and nonjudgmental. It is a conscious choice I make every day. It is not automatic and it is not always easy. But when you practice this long enough, it gets easier.

It works! It works in every situation, from interactions with your spouse and family to coworkers, teammates, even in political and corporate settings. It is simple but not easy.

To be honest it can feel as if you are the only one willing to make concessions in an argument, and that can become discouraging. The more you put aside judging and assuming, the less you will betray yourself, and that is the reward we are after.

The first step is to recognize that you are judging. That in itself is a task, as sometimes we are not aware that we are judging.

The transformation starts with becoming curious about everything we experience in a day. This also means we work on fewer assumptions. This way we teach ourselves to operate from a different mindset.

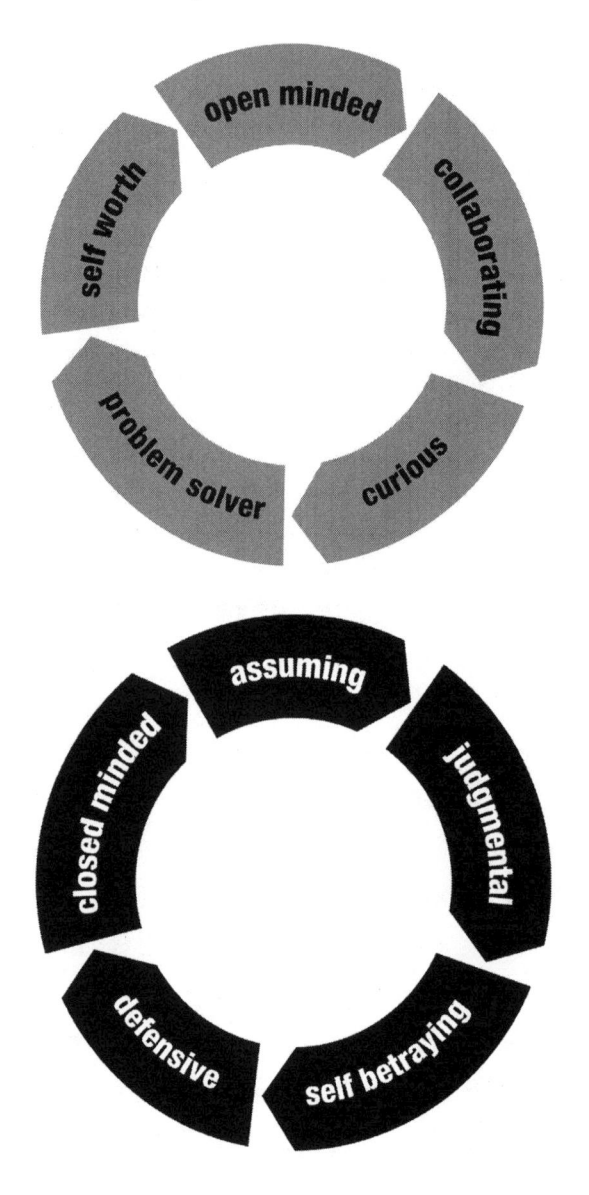

When you look at the previous graphs, you can see the differences in mindsets. Now it is up to you to choose which one you want to have. Don't let anyone tell you there is no choice, because that is not the truth.

You can measure the level of judging and assuming you do, and once you change that, you can measure your level of open mindedness and curiosity. The choice is yours and yours alone.

Miscommunication

All the causes of conflict we've discussed in this chapter combine to create in the final cause - misinterpreted communication or miscommunications.

It is little wonder so much goes wrong with communicating when you take into consideration all the elements that are involved. From personal stress, assumptions and judgments, to underlying beliefs that influence our choices that we may not even are aware of. Little wonder communication is one of the most difficult skills to develop as a human being.

But it is the most important one.

However, when we choose an open mindset when dealing with others, we may think we are clear in our communication, but if the receiver doesn't feel the same way, we are already miss communicating. It is helpful to have the person you are talking with, repeat back to you what they heard you say or you can repeat back to them what you believe they said. This gives you the chance to explain more if you find out that they didn't get your point.

This may seem like the longer route, but it will save on all the extra time and energy you would spend on resolving conflict and clearing up misunderstandings.

Summary

- ✓ Conflict can make you grow and push you out your comfort zone, and that can be healthy, if you let it.
- ✓ Conflict is inevitable, and the mindset you choose will determine how you deal with the causes of conflict.
- ✓ Conflict is caused by:
- ✓ Personal stress
- ✓ Taking everything personally
- ✓ Making judgments
- ✓ Making assumptions
- ✓ Betraying yourself
- ✓ Personal responsibilities
- ✓ Family and societal culture
- ✓ Misinterpreted communication
- ✓ We have different coping mechanisms:
- ✓ Avoiding the issue
- ✓ Dismissing the issue
- ✓ Being closed off

- ✓ Acting like a martyr or victim
- ✓ Attacking or being confrontational
- ✓ Always keep in mind that betraying yourself creates conflict within yourself and therefore conflict with others.
- ✓ Always ask powerful questions and be curious.

CHAPTER 4

Accountability

Now that we have looked at trust and conflict and what that does for a healthy relationship, it is time to look at the next part of the five-point system - accountability.

The definition of accountability, according to the Canadian Oxford Dictionary, is responsible; required to account for one's conduct.

What does that mean exactly? We touched on being responsible in the previous chapter, and now it is time to really analyze it. To practice clear communication, when I talk about responsibility, I mean that you are responsible for your thoughts, everything you say, and everything you do.

Let this statement seep into every fiber of your being because this is a crucial step in connecting to your **I Am status**. You can't operate from your pure being if somebody else is in control of your life. With control comes a responsibility.

When we do take responsibility for ourselves, we can stop blaming others. Taking responsibility results in less stress and conflict.

However, being accountable is like an iceberg, the biggest portion of your responsibility is under the surface. The piece of the iceberg we see is our accountability toward others. Underwater is our responsibility toward our self. A healthy iceberg is 10 percent above water and 90 percent underwater.

Can you say the same about your responsibility?

With accountability, 10 percent is toward others, and 90 percent is responsibility toward yourself. Often this is reversed. We devote 90 percent of our time and responsibility to others and 10 percent toward ourselves.

The beauty of this ratio is that whatever goes wrong in our lives, we can on blame somebody else because it is their responsibility, not ours.

This happens all around us, which is understandable since that is what we teach our children. We shelter them from making mistakes because their mistakes don't make us look like good parents. Some mistakes can be forgiven, but what about a failure?

Fear of Failure

Ever noticed that Western society frowns upon failure? Many people are afraid of failure and all because we've made failure look like the end of the world. We call those who fail a loser, a dumb person. Instead of admitting to a mistake or a failure, it's easier to turn around and blame others for our blunders.

The sad part is in this society we get away with that, on all levels from personal interaction to the education system to government. Everybody blames everybody else except themselves.

I'm not promoting blaming yourself, because that is good for nothing but putting yourself down. What I want to do is wake people up and make them aware of the choices they have. We don't have to follow the crowd.

We all are unique beings, like every iceberg is different but majestic in its own way. We choose how to flow.

How to Hold Yourself Accountable

When I surveyed people, asking them, "How do you see yourself when you are held accountable for your actions? the responses varied. Most people answered, "I take full responsibility for all my actions." (73.2%). The second most popular response was other and 14.6% of those who responded answered, "Most of the time events happen, and I just react to them."

Q7: How do you see yourself when you are held accountable for your actions?

I take full responsibility for all my actions.	73.2%	30
Most of the time events happen, and I just react to them.	14.6%	6
Other	24.4%	10
		Answered question 41
		skipped question 1

(Survey conducted courtesy of SurveyMonkey Inc.)[6]

"Other" responses:

1. I seek responsibility and go slow reactivity, so that I can better understand myself and what's going on.
2. Look in the mirror.
3. I take responsibility for what I have done, sometimes it is a misunderstanding too and have found it important to even clear up what was perceived to have happened.
4. Nobody likes to be wrong but it is important to be able to stand up and say "Yes, I was wrong." Learn from it and move on. Accountability of people's actions is one of my favorite things to

[6] Ibid.

see. I am always proud when my son or my staffs is accountable for their actions. It makes it easier for me to move forward knowing that have stepped up and chances are will never make that mistake again. I admire people who are strong enough to stand up and say they were wrong.
5. Most of the time I take full responsibility but sometimes I just react.
6. Something in between.
7. I do react in some instances, but upon reflection will determine if I could have done things differently. If so, I will prepare myself with possible solutions that could be used if a similar situation were to arise in the future.
8. An opportunity to learn something.
9. A combination of the two.
10. I try to take full responsibility but fail to do so on occasion.

As we can see from the survey, people want to be held accountable for their actions. Some of us make a conscious choice to take steps ensuring others know that we take accountability seriously.

What would happen if we used and saw accountability as a learning tool?

We could take responsibility for something that went wrong or not as planned and turn it around and say, "That didn't turn out well, so I won't do it this way again."

I was seventeen and talking to my cousin who was thirty and married. I asked her why they hadn't had children yet in a somewhat rude and assuming way. The cousin replied that it was not by choice and that they were having some trouble conceiving. With the answer, the cousin let me know that my assumptions and rather direct question might have hurt her feelings. I was very was embarrassed, but the cousin replied in such a nice, undefensive way it did not judge me, just recognized my youth and inexperience. I never acted that way again. I learned a valuable lesson from my cousin's answer.

So why does it seem that many of us don't step up to the plate and be accountable for our actions? I think the following poem provides some insight.

> Watch your thoughts, they become words;
> Watch your words, they become actions;
> Watch your actions, they become habits;
> Watch your habits, they become character;
> Watch your character, for it becomes your destiny."

FRANK OUTLAW
Late President of the Bi-Lo Stores

Everything we react to and feel starts with what and how we think in that particular moment. When we want to take responsibility in a relationship, we have to start with how we think. If you think you can't control what you think, then you are mistaken.

At first thoughts seem to just drift in our heads with no direction; they come in and go out. But as we start pondering them, we take them as the truth. This process is done subconsciously, happening in just seconds.

Meditation

Now what would happen if we brought this process to the conscious mind?

This is exactly what meditation does. When you meditate, you focus on the breath, and when you focus on the breath, thoughts will pop up in your mind. The purpose of meditation is to let the thoughts flow through the mind without stopping them or questioning them. It is like passing a car without paying attention to what kind of car it is, who is driving, where it is going, how many are in the car, or even what color it is. You just pass the car, not noticing the details and move on.

Meditation has many positive effects. As you slow your thinking process, you are not as quick to react or judge. Doing this helps you handle conflict in a healthy way.

There are many good books on meditation if you want to try it. I enjoyed <u>Search Inside Yourself</u> by Chade-Meng Tad. It clearly explains meditation and mindfulness. Chade-Meng Tad highlights all the benefits and includes instructions. He jokes that if he and other engineers can do it, you can do it.

When we meditate, we bring our deepest beliefs to the surface of our consciousness. As discussed in Chapter 1, we have many deep-rooted beliefs that we learned as kids and took on as truth. Beliefs about money, self-worth and the importance of pleasing parents and family are just a few examples of truths we believe in without thinking about why or their source.

By paying attention to your thoughts you can start to unravel your own thinking and belief systems. Meditation allows you to exam your beliefs and see if they are still true for you. If they are, you know you can trust this belief because it is part of your makeup.

Questioning Your Core Beliefs

Since I was four I wanted to be a farmer. Even though I'm now pursuing a different path, I'm still a farmer at heart, and I always will be. That is why my focus is on healthy family team building, especially for family businesses, which is what most farms are.

I'm fascinated by how we move from a parent-child relationship to being partners in business. That is not an easy transition, not for the parents who have to give control over to the "child" (who by then is twenty or older) and not for the child who is afraid to fail the business and therefore the parents.

This applies not just to families in business but to all families. Parents have to accept that their children are adults and they will make their own decisions, even when the parents don't agree with those choices.

What should you do when you find out that what you always believed is not true for you? That is a loaded question because when you ask this question, you already know something doesn't feel right. The courageous will look at this belief and try to unravel where it came from.

This sounds easy, but it can be messy, heart-rending, and difficult.

It is all too easy to blame your parents or your circumstances for your actions (which are connected to what you believe).

Blame often leads to feelings of guilt and shame. When you are in the blaming mindset, it is difficult to look at the issue from different perspectives. Your actions and reactions are the result of the perspective you are in at that moment.

The first thing to do when examining your beliefs is to let go of blaming others for where you are at. When you blame somebody or something, you view yourself as a victim and therefore don't take responsibility for your thoughts and actions. You don't take control of your life.

There are situations where people are victims, but even when you are a victim, you don't have to behave as one and get stuck in that perspective. It is not the situation of being a victim that can hold you back, but your behavior as a victim.

Questioning your beliefs may feel as if you are betraying your parents, partners or others. Feelings of being misunderstood, not good enough, not valuable or worthy are just a few examples of the types of negative thoughts that will emerge, and you need to face them before you can put them to rest.

What about guilt? Parents sometimes use guilt to convey to their children what they want them to do. My mom used it, and if I'm honest, I used it on my own children once or twice when they were growing up.

Why do we use this trick? Because we know that most of the time it works because children don't want to disappoint their parents but it has a downfall as a parenting technique. Using guilt in this way creates insecurity in the way we validate ourselves. Controlling someone by shaming them does the same thing. When shame and guilt are strongly present in our beings, it is harder, and for some impossible, to take control of our own lives. Guilt and shame creates feelings of not being good enough, smart enough, and beautiful enough or just enough and these feeling can rule our lives and actions with their lies.

It is no surprise that these feelings also become trust issues, responsibility issues and create unhealthy conflict. Therefore, I recommend against using the guilt-trip technique on children, because guilt often changes into feelings of shame and blame, which will undermine children's self-esteem. The damage that guilt does is often invisible till years later when the children are grown-ups and on their own.

Giving & Receiving Feedback

As adults we try to hide our insecurities behind masks of confidence. This works until something unexpected happens and we need to deal with a conflict, personal responsibility, giving our trust or making a commitment. Our insecurities come to the surface and play a role in how we react and how we receive feedback on our performance and behavior.

Most of us are defensive when anything about us is judged or identified. We create excuses to justify our behavior. This reaction indicates that the person feels their self-worth is being attacked. Although that may not be the intention of the one giving the feedback, the reaction will be instinctive and sometimes harsh. This can snowball into an argument or a fight, when the responsibility of an action is questioned.

Survey responses to the question, "How do you react when peers comment on your performance and behavior?" provide insight on how to give good feedback without upsetting the recipient.

The better you are at giving constructive feedback, the better you become at receiving it. Even when someone gives feedback in an awkward way, you may instinctively know that your colleague does not mean harm. They just don't know how to give good feedback.

Most respondents have a conversation about the comment (69%) Those who don't want to damage the relationship, brush over the conversation (14.3%). Some people tune them out (4.8%)

Q8: How do you react when peers comment on your performance and behavior?

I tune them out.	4.8%	2
I have a conversation about the comment.	69.0%	29
I do everything possible to avoid a conversation.	0.0%	0
I don't want to damage the relationship, so I brush over the conversation.	14.3%	6
Other	21.4%	9
		Answered question 42
		Skipped question 1

(Survey conducted courtesy of SurveyMonkey Inc.)[7]

---

[7] Ibid.

"Other" responses:

1. I try to listen to what they are telling me, though it depends who is calling me on my actions, I trust some more on their opinions then others.
2. Probably all of the above at one time or another. Typically, I stay and try to understand, then work through feelings privately (or with a friend) if the situation feels too vulnerable (and not safe).
3. Look inwards to see if there is correctness in their comments. See if behavior should change. Stew about it afterward.
4. Good to see what others see too at times as we can be blind sighted.
5. I listen to their comments and take the comments seriously.
6. I think about it and try to get better. I question peers to find out how.
7. This seems to assume that the comment is negative?
8. As tough as it is to hear criticism about one's behavior, I try to brace myself for the worst, hear what the person has to say and will defend myself if they are wrong. Otherwise I try to ask questions to determine why they think what they think so that I can improve. But I must

stress here that again that it depends on what else is going on in my life, at that time, and how important what they're saying really is. For instance, if it's about my leaving a dirty dish somewhere, they are being petty. If it's about the way I have treated them, then I had better do something about it. Their approach is probably more important than what they are saying.
9. Depending on whom it is/the situation.

The majority of the respondents have enough self-compassion to engage in a talk about how others perceive them. I found especially interesting this comment: "Their approach is probably more important than what they are saying."

My conclusion is that most of us are open to comments on our performances or behaviors, as long as people do it respectfully and without a hidden agenda, such as back-stabbing or putting us down. This reinforces my belief that we need to feel validated first before we take on accountability.

What can you do to give the most nonthreatening feedback possible?

Pay attention to where the person is at emotionally. If you see the individual is mad, sad, or overwhelmed, then the chances are small that he or she is open for receiving comments. In cases like that, wait for the person's mood to change before you make your comment. If that is not possible, then first acknowledge the emotion you see and ask some powerful questions to try to create a more settled mood or different state of mind and make the atmosphere more open and receiving. Check in with yourself and note your mood and state of mind.

Keep in mind that if you can read somebody else's mood, they can read you. Feedback you give while feeling frustrated and close-minded will never be well-received. It will seem as if you are attacking as opposed to giving well-meaning comments. This is another contributor to conflict.

Feedback Checklist

Before giving constructive feedback, pay attention to this checklist:

- ✓ What is the emotional state of the receiver? Is he or she ready to listen?
- ✓ Is this the right time and place to give feedback?
- ✓ Can I give feedback with focus, ease, and grace right now?
- ✓ What steps can I take to step back if the moment becomes too heated?
- ✓ What is needed in this moment to give and receive honest, open-minded feedback? (For

example: Do I need to take a couple of deep breaths before I say something? Do I need to walk in the garden before I start?)
- ✓ Am I viewing and treating feedback as a learning opportunity, or as a dumping ground for the negative thoughts I may have?

This may seem like an extensive checklist, but the more you practice this, the easier it becomes. The good news is you can use this in every conversation you have and with everybody you know. These tips will decrease the amount of conflict you encounter in life, and help you become better able to deal with it.

Ideally, if everybody followed the checklist, there would be less conflict in the world. Everybody would be paying attention to others and waiting to discuss issues until the receiving party was ready, willing, and able. What a utopia that would be.

However, we are all humans with our own insecurities and bad days. So the question isn't what we do if we fall off the bandwagon but when. We all have days when we don't feel diplomatic, because of life events. What the issue is, doesn't matter, the only thing that matters is how you recover from it.

Your choices are:

- ✓ You can stick your head in the sand and pretend nothing happened, which will create friction and make the issue fester until it bursts again.
- ✓ After a cooling-off period you take responsibility and apologize for your actions.
- ✓ You apologize and forgive everybody involved, including yourself. People often forget or struggle with this option. It's not that we don't want to forgive; it's more we don't know how.

Understanding Forgiveness

We don't fully understand what forgiveness means. Maybe between all of us we can get a broader perspective on what forgiveness means for people individually. When I asked people to complete the sentence, "For me to forgive someone is to:" the most frequently picked response was "To let go of the resentment and anger." (72.1%)

Over 39.5%, responded forgiveness was "To try to separate between the person and the things he or she did that hurt me." The least common reply (7%) was "Just forget all the things the other person did to me even when they really hurt me."

The "Other" responses (14%) were:

To express the hurt, anger, resentment (even if meditatively), to seek to understand the WHY (not just what happened), to seek to understand what "in you" allowed that to happen (low esteem, poor self-image, etc, and then to forgive (let them go) and be embraced with love.

Q1: For me to forgive someone is to:

Just forget all the things the other person did to me even when they really hurt me.	7.0%	3
To let go of the resentment and anger.	72.1%	31
To try to separate between the person and the things he or she did that hurt me.	39.5%	17
Other	14.0%	6
		Answered question 43
		skipped question 0

(Survey conducted courtesy of SurveyMonkey Inc.)[8]

---

[8] Ibid.

"Other" responses:

1. To express the hurt, anger, resentment (even if meditatively), to seek to understand the WHY (not just what happened), to seek to understand what "in you" allowed that to happen (low esteem, poor self-image, ect(*sic*), and then to forgive (let them go) and be embraced with love.
2. See them as someone that is human. People make mistakes even if they are repetitious. Everyone has life lessons and to let go is to be free yourself of that negativity in your soul.
3. Restore the good relationship with that person and to be able to love that person for who he or she is.
4. To forgive is to bring ease to the forgiven's mind and my own as well.
5. It's about releasing any connection between the injured/hurt person and the event that requires the disconnections. It is not to forget what happened in the sense that you will not allow it to happen again.
6. To learn from the experience so I don't get "burned" in the same way again and to express genuine gratitude for the knowledge/wisdom I gained from the experience.

As you can see, there are many different ways to view forgiveness. There is no right or wrong way. When I read those comments, I think that although our lives are filled with painful events that confront us with dark feelings like blame, shame, and guilt, we can refuse to let our lives be dictated by them.

We may honestly believe that we refuse to let our lives be dictated by painful events, but is that the truth? If you're asking this question, it implies that you are already searching for your own inner truth.

It is time to really break down what forgiveness is and what it is not. Forgiveness is breaking the attachment we have to feelings of anger, blame, resentment, and judgment toward others and ourselves that are created by life experiences we perceive as hurtful.

With forgiveness we operate from, are in touch and in control of the **I Am status.** Being in this state frees us to move forward in life without getting tangled in the hurdles of unfinished business.

When we refuse to deal with hard feelings and experiences, and push them to the backs of our minds, we are just putting it all into a backpack we have to carry. It may be out of sight, but it won't be out of mind, because the heaviness will slow us down. Over time we often forget what baggage we have, but that baggage still influences our life decisions.

Visualize Forgiveness

Imagine you are walking in a meadow. The sun is shining, the grass is green under your feet, and the trees are slowly waving in the breeze. It is warm enough to walk in a T-shirt, and the birds are chirping. There is a peace all around you.

This is your core, you're **I Am status**. The beauty and the tranquility fuel your walk of life. This is the base for your life force. It is the measuring point of what makes you happy and gives you the drive and courage to move forward.

Now the meadow is changing. Clouds roll in, in the form of health issues, money problems, or relationship disruptions. Events occur in which you are confronted with your insecurities, and all of a sudden the landscape of the meadow is different. You feel thrown off-course, threatened by the unknown, maybe even lost. You feel disconnected from yourself. You are carrying a heavy backpack that you've tried to hide all the "negative" life events and experiences in so that you don't see them. Even as you try creating the illusion that you are still walking in the sunny, peaceful meadow, it feels like a lie.

Most people put those bad experiences in the backpack. At times, this can be helpful, especially when something has impacted our life immediately in one way or another. Veterans from different wars and on all sides did and still do this. All first responders have examples of doing this.

Forgiving Yourself

My heart and compassion is with all of you on the front lines. Hopefully this book helps you find the strength and courage to move forward in life without carrying your full gear.

People experience personal hell. I went through my own personal hell when my water broke when I was only twenty-one weeks along with my son. It was so sudden that I went into survival mode. I went through the motions without really paying attention and looking at my deeper feelings. My focus was on the sunny meadow, even when I was confronted with questions like - Will I have to bury my baby? How far will we take the neonatal care? What will be the life expectancy for my baby? I was dealing with chronically sick kids and now my pregnancy was in jeopardy. The only thing I felt that I could do was take it one day at a time. All my unsolved "negative" emotions swirled through me. As if I didn't have enough to deal with, people were giving me advice on what I should and shouldn't do. I knew they meant well, but it was useless for me at the time.

The future felt unsure. I was assaulted by fear and feelings of guilt. What if I didn't follow some advice? Maybe those people were right? To cope, I stashed all the upsetting thoughts into my backpack. I operated from what I knew at that time, the beliefs and thoughts that I'd learned in childhood and from all the other important people in my life. The life experiences of people I admired, like Sue and Will, who dealt with their life challenges with grace. But I didn't really deal with my grief at the time - I put it in my backpack.

Even though my pregnancy was difficult, my unborn child flourished. He grew on target with a strong heartbeat. All the ultrasounds were good. The natural-birth delivery was over in two and a half hours. When he was born, all was finally well.

You would think that all those negative, scary feelings I put in my backpack disappeared because it was all over.

Wrong. It was not that simple. You eventually have to face your emotions. I finally dealt with mine five months after Peter was born. A neighbor delivered a son who had a heart defect, and he died two days later. She didn't even know there was anything wrong with the baby until he was born.

When we went to the visitation at their house, all my bottled-up fear, grief and pain came rushing out. I cried and cried. I felt such deep grief for that couple. I saw the reality of burying your child.

When I look back at this part of my life, I only feel gratitude and no unresolved feelings. I know all the negative emotions are out of my backpack, replaced with grace and forgiveness. After my breakdown at the neighbor's I understood that I also had to forgive myself.

I had felt guilty being in the hospital on bed rest while my husband looked after our two boys and ran the farm. I had to forgive myself for being self-centered at times and not paying attention to the needs and wants of the people around me. I had to forgive my body for not being perfect and in good working order. I also had to forgive friends and family members for not being there for me when I needed them most.

That is what looking in your backpack is all about. With forgiveness comes grace and gratitude for the things that passed.

Let's clarify one thing: forgiveness doesn't mean that you have to forget all the disempowering things a person did to you. It only means that you refuse to carry all the negative results of that situation with you. Forgiveness lightens your backpack and nobody else's. The other person has to forgive themselves to be free of the situation. That is not your responsibility.

We all carry a backpack and have gone through our own personal hells. I encourage you to empty your backpack and start traveling light. It will make your life much easier. Start with becoming aware of your **I Am status**, and look for the **I Am status** in others. That's where you will find the act of forgiving.

Forgiving Others

Forgiveness is not burying, forgetting, or excusing events that happened to us. We forgive because we must acknowledge the wrong that was committed.

Forgiveness does not allow or excuse hurtful behaviors, nor does it allow it to continue. It cannot be used to excuse or ignore past or future hurtful behavior. Forgiving someone doesn't automatically mean you have to keep this person in your life, which will always be a difficult choice we need to make.

Do we always have to inform the person if we decide to forgive them? And if yes, how does this work if that person is far away, you don't want contact with him or her, or he or she is deceased?

Most of the time you can forgive someone without making personal contact. There are different ways to do this. You need to find one that works for you. You could book some sessions with a psychologist or a life coach. You could write a letter to the person about your feelings, the anger and frustration. Then instead of sending it, rip it up or burn it. Writing the letter is a way of getting your emotions outside of you so that it is easier for you to let the negativity go. The beauty of it is that you can do this over and over again until you find that the attached emotion is gone without confrontation or doing yourself harm.

Going through a forgiveness affair and then letting it go can be difficult and challenging, but remember, carrying a heavy, heavy backpack will slow you down and hurt you in ways that reach all aspects and all interactions of your life.

As with all skills, practice makes perfect. And all of us can get as much practice as we want because there will be no shortness of opportunity. By practicing forgiveness we are building the muscle that helps us see others as whole people, their greatness and their challenges. As you tone your forgiveness muscle and practice looking at the whole person with compassion, please don't forget to do the same for yourself. You are just as important as the next person.

Gratitude

Self-worth also comes with gratitude. We explored forgiveness already, but I think we need to spend some time on gratitude.

Gratitude is another word that sounds so familiar that we think we know what it means. It is also a big word (maybe some of us are even a little bit afraid of it) because it implies you have to say thank you and be good.

Now here is the thing: you can be grateful for a lot of things. Many things to be grateful for don't cost much. Some are free.

When I surveyed people and asked, "What makes you happy and smile (show gratitude)?" the most popular response was my family (81%), followed by my friends (73.8%). Sunshine and people smiling tied at 71.4%, while 54.8% answered my job and fall weather was picked by 47.6%. Coffee from Tim Horton's and Starbuck's was selected by 19% of respondents.

(Q10: What makes you happy and smile (show gratitude)?

Your job	54.8%	23
Your family	81.0%	34
Your friends	73.8%	31
Coffee from Tim Horton's / Starbucks	19.0%	8
Sunshine	71.4%	30
People smiling	71.4%	30
Fall weather	47.6%	20
Other	31.0%	13
		Answered question 42
		skipped question 1

(Survey conducted courtesy of SurveyMonkey Inc.)[9]

---

[9] Ibid.

"Other" responses:

1. Look on the bright side. There are enough sourpusses around.
2. Life in general.
3. All of the above, I love life! Also love going out with friends and family, love to worship and be in church full of his life.
4. I think it is important to get joy out of everything you do. I try and not take things for granted. A ray of sunshine is a beautiful thing. A rainbow. Stars at night. My dog waiting at the door for me. My son's smile. All little things but we stop and really think of all the beauty and wondrous things in our lives, however small, we could all have happy moments through the day, even if our job is getting us down, or our kids are getting on our nerves. It's the little things that always make me smile and happy.
5. Outdoor activities.
6. When I experience good things / deeds that make the world (also at a small scale) a better place.
7. Exercise.
8. My grandchildren.
9. Exercise praising GOD.

10. My GOD is the one thing that makes me happy. He is my salvation and the only true purpose in life. He causes me to see things the way I should see them and hopefully not the way I think I should see them.
11. Happy animals and peaceful images or surroundings.
12. Feeling purposeful.
13. My dogs. Tea. Yoga, working out. Music. Snow.

Getting organized. Learning new things. Helping. Joking around.

What a great, long list! I trust that there were at least a couple examples you could relate to. If you can be grateful for all the beautiful little or big things in life, your life is just a bit brighter. By focusing on authentic gratitude you automatically step into your **I Am status,** which translates into increased levels of optimism, energy, empathy, and compassion. And all simply by paying attention to the everyday wonderful things around you. Don't kid yourself, there is always something to be thankful for, even the fact that you are breathing.

The rest of your life may be challenging and difficult, but you can always find a silver lining in a dark cloud.

Often we don't understand the impact we have on others. If everybody would pay forward one act of kindness a day, the world would be a better place.

One way to express gratitude is by saying thank you while looking people in the eyes so they know it is sincere gratitude and not just politeness. When a stranger holds a door open for me, I always look them in the eyes and say thank you.

You should also show gratitude for waitresses and others who serve you. Your acknowledge them as a person and not merely an extension of the environment, making the person feel valued.

They pay such kindnesses forward by passing on your kindness, by going out of their way for someone else.

Calling or sending a card to someone is another way of expressing gratitude, and people often greatly appreciate this personal action. Silent gratitude may be the most difficult form of expressing thankfulness. With this method you express your thankfulness and send it into the universe just by thinking about it.

This is difficult because you don't see any immediate reaction from your gratitude. Silent gratitude is often the most forgotten and least favorite way of saying thank you. Simply saying thank you to the universe in a sincere way is the start of a prayer. There is no protocol on how to do this right. You can't do it wrong. When a feeling of gratitude hits, just stop your thoughts, consciously feel the gratitude, say Thank you out loud or in silence. After that pay attention what comes up for you. You may experience another breakthrough thought or feel at peace.

You can choose to express silent gratitude at a special time of the day, or whenever you think about something or someone. When hurt or pain engulfs you and yet you can still find something to be learned from those troubles, please be grateful for that, because that's how you measure your growth.

I could write a book on accountability alone. As we discovered, accountability is the umbrella for responsibility, forgiveness, feedback, blame, shame, guilt, and gratitude.

Summary

- ✓ You are responsible for your thoughts, words, actions, habits, and therefore destiny.
- ✓ When you take full responsibility, you will connect and operate more from your **I Am status**.
- ✓ Being accountable is like an iceberg: 10 percent is toward others and 90 percent is toward yourself.
- ✓ Hanging on to blame, shame, and guilt prevents us from moving forward in our lives and does more damage than we realize.
- ✓ Giving constructive feedback is an art.
- ✓ Don't take everything personally when receiving feedback.
- ✓ Tone and body language are crucial tools for delivering feedback in a way that will be received with an open mind.

- Forgiveness is an act of courage and compassion.
- Forgiveness is a key to happiness and inner peace.
- Not forgiving is like a wall between two beings. It can become too thick and high to conquer. When that happens, your flow of life, as well as the other person's, is disturbed.
- Only you can forgive yourself and the other, and that is your responsibility.
- Forgiveness can occur by talking about it, writing a letter and then burning it, having a meditative "talk" with the person and letting it go into the universe, or using whatever method works for you.
- Gratitude is a deep emotion that you tap into when you express your appreciation for what you have.
- Gratitude is a key element for inner peace and long-lasting happiness.
- By practicing gratitude you live in the present moment and are connected to your **I Am status**.
- See the beauty and the lessons in all the "negative" life events you encounter.
- Say thank you for all the life lessons you receive.
- Practice gratitude every day by writing what you are grateful for and calling or saying thank you to somebody each day.

CHAPTER 5

Commitment

In this chapter we will look at the next level in relationships - commitment to relationships, careers, and causes.

If you view trust, accountability, and conflict as building blocks for any interaction we have, then commitment is the glue holding relationships together. If there is no glue, your relationship is easily knocked over. This holds true for all relationships including causes you are passionate about, and your heart's desire.

The definition of commitment, from the Canadian Oxford Dictionary, is "the process or an instance of committing oneself; pledge or undertaking. An engagement or obligation that restricts freedom of action."

What is the impact of this word on our daily interactions with each other?

When people were asked, "When you hear the word commitment, what comes to mind?" most people surveyed answered "Needing to trust first before committing something (51.2%). The second most popular response was "Other" where they supplied their own definitions of commitment. Around 24.4% of the people surveyed defined commitment as "Making decisions," while 17.1% believed it was "Needing to know all angles to make a decision. For 4.9% of respondents, commitment meant, "Always making the right decision."

Q11: When you hear the word commitment, what comes to mind?

Making decisions	24.4%	10
Always making the right decisions	4.9%	2
Needing to know all angles to make a decision	17.1%	7
Needing to trust first before committing to something	51.2%	21
Other	26.8%	11
		Answered question 41
		skipped question 2

(Survey conducted courtesy of SurveyMonkey Inc.)[10]

---

[10] Ibid.

"Other" responses:

1. To "stay with" a process or a person or a choice as an act of love. When it stops being an act of love, it is no longer a commitment.
2. It means to fully support something even if initially I disagreed with it. I will support it and work towards it.
3. Commitment makes me wonder if I can give the time for such an arrangement. If I believe in the commitment enough, I will make the time to be involved and do the best that I can with full focus.
4. We are not to commit to everything, we are to prioritize.
5. Involvement, stand by your promises and goals.
6. Seeing totally devoted to something. All action decisions are made with whatever/whoever you are committing to.
7. Making a decision or choice and following through with it even if it becomes hard.
8. Commitment means long-term loyalty to a decision I've made.
9. Doing what I say I am going to do.
10. Commitment is the ultimate agreement. I want to be prepared to NOT go back on my word.
11. Aligning your heart and your mind for something.

12. Decisions based on truth (soul directed).

I'm so grateful that people took the time to fill out this survey, so that I could share a broader view and multiple personal perspectives on commitment. Commitment is a serious topic for everyone.

There were many questions about commitment that I didn't ask. Some of them are:

- ✓ Are all commitments we make the same?
- ✓ Why might we break a commitment?
- ✓ What are the consequences when we break a commitment?
- ✓ What is needed to honor a commitment?

There are many things to consider when discussing commitment. When we hear or read the word commitment, we believe that we know what we are talking about but commitment is a complicated subject that makes complicated feelings and reaction arise. By examining the following questions, we will add more dimension to our understanding of what it means.

Are all the commitments we make the same?

We can debate the answer to that, especially if we look clinically at the word commitment. Some of us will say they are the same, and others will say they aren't.

I recognize three types of commitment we use every day, even if we aren't aware of it, and we use different standards for these different types of commitment:

- ✓ Commitment to self, which is connected to the **I Am status.**
- ✓ Commitment to other relationships.
- ✓ Commitment to a cause.

What are the ingredients in the superglue of commitment?

- ✓ Trust,
- ✓ Love,
- ✓ Responsibility,
- ✓ Vulnerability,
- ✓ Loyalty.

With the right mixture of ingredients we can create a strong commitment to all three different kinds of commitment.

But what do we actually use the glue for?

We use the glue to fuse two or more relationship building blocks together to create a shared vision. Other components may be: passion, confidence, courage, choice, willingness, and focus.

Commitment to Self

If any of the ingredients are missing, the glue is compromised. Life involves making compromises. But if something has to give, most often, we choose to compromise on a commitment we made to ourselves.

This is the most damaging choice in the long run. You betray yourself over and over again. These repeated actions bury your **I Am status** under illusions. The more personal commitments you violate, the more you stop trusting yourself. Your self-esteem falters and feelings of betrayal become your constant companion. You begin to spiral downward.

What makes it so difficult to keep our commitments to ourselves?

When we make a commitment, we force ourselves to take responsibility for change in our lives. Most people are afraid of change.

Like water, we take the path of least resistance. If we can go around an obstacle we will, even if it is not in our best interests or the best interests of a higher cause. The obstacle brings change, whether that obstacle is our personal belief system, self-esteem, not following the crowd, going against loved ones' wishes, life events etc.

Personal commitment rarely includes accountability to someone else. No outside accountability makes it easier to break or not follow through on the commitment you have made to yourself. When we have betrayed ourselves, our thinking ability is compromised. This is a challenge we all face. But it is not inevitable and can be fixed.

Your **I Am status** is your authentic, calm, secure, loving inner voice. When you feel frustrated, overwhelmed, challenged, attacked, or insecure, it is not your **I Am voice** speaking. It is another voice.

Self-Sabotage (aka the Saboteur)

Self-sabotage is known by life coaches, writers, artists as the saboteur, the gremlin or monkey mind. The trick is to understand clearly from whom your thoughts originate. Our **I Am status** thoughts are clear, positive, calm and loving.

Who is the saboteur and what do those thoughts feel like?

Your saboteur is similar to a stage director, who thinks he is in charge of your life. The saboteur is with us from the moment we come into this world and will leave us the moment we pass on. Their main goal is to create a stage performance (life) full of drama, misery, and chaos. Your saboteur interprets every movement you make, tells you what to do, what to think, how to behave, and what to believe.

Your saboteur will do everything in his power to stop the main character (you) from overcoming life's challenges and tapping into your brilliant self, the **I Am status.**

This is done through thoughts that reference past failures or worrying about your future. Saboteur thoughts don't linger in the present, because that's where the **I Am status** is the most powerful. The more off balanced you are, the more powerful your saboteur is. View your saboteur as a bad actor who will do anything to get and keep the spotlight.

How Does Your Saboteur Take Control

- ✓ By telling you what you should and shouldn't do.
- ✓ By telling you that you are not good enough, smart enough, strong enough, or brilliant enough to survive on your own.
- ✓ By putting roadblocks up.
- ✓ By pointing out what can go wrong.
- ✓ By keeping you away from personal growth. The smaller you are, the more power he has.
- ✓ By pushing you to do better than telling you that you will never have enough money, power, etc.
- ✓ By telling you that you have too much and that you should be satisfied with less, making you assume the role of a victim or a martyr.
- ✓ By blaming, shaming, and making you feel guilty.

- ✓ By ignoring situations or uncomfortable thoughts because what you don't see it, you don't question and you don't confront, won't change.

Think seriously about the techniques your saboteur thoughts use to keep you small. Write them down. You are exposing your saboteur, not letting him lurk in the shadows.

Identifying Your Saboteur

The moment you know the techniques being used, the more visible your saboteur becomes to you. If you recognize the way you are allowing sabotaging thoughts to hold you back, the quicker you can sidestep them. But first, you need to become more familiar with your sabotaging sidekick.

When Your Saboteur Shows Up

Whenever you want to change your behavior, question your beliefs, or honor your personal commitments, your saboteur rings an inner alarm system. These alarms come in different shapes and sizes.

An alarm can be the voice of your parents in your head or feelings of fear and uneasiness. When these alarms of false fear show up, your saboteur thoughts pretend to "save" you from losing a relationship, making a poor career choice, or some other catastrophe.

Do you recognize thoughts like "I'm not good enough," "This will never work," "I can't do that," or "Who am I to say something?" These are your personal saboteur thoughts. We all have a saboteur. If you think you don't have one that is the first clue you do.

Sabotaging thoughts keep the status quo, they allow no change. But life is all about changes. Most people fear that reality. When a change is about to take place, the sabotaging thoughts are on high alert, doing and saying anything to prevent you from accepting and enjoying changes.

For young, new parents the loss of personal time and adjusting to new responsibilities takes its toll on relationships. With empty-nest parents, the change from looking after their children to having no children to care for creates a void. They forget who they were on their own, and don't know what to do when they have just themselves to look after. They have to let their adult kids make their own mistakes, while they try to find who they are now. Other big changes include changing careers, moving to a different city or country. Many changes we face in our lifetimes look more like threats than opportunities. Living with fear controlling your decisions results in forgetting and losing contact with your inner values.

You make decisions from the saboteur point of view and not from your brilliant **I Am status**.

It becomes a big problem when interacting with people. You must consider, are you communicating with the true person or their saboteur? A trained life coach can determine the origin of your thoughts by your voice. When your saboteur is talking, your tone is flatter and defensive, or the saboteur tries to reason its way out of the situation/conversation. When your true self is talking, your voice is light, bright, and enthusiastic. Even when a situation is sad, you can still be your true self. When a person shows up as genuine, authentic, and listening in Level 3, then it is the true person you are communicating with. Their sabotaging thoughts are locked in the closet.

We all have moments when we communicate from our **I Am status**. Just think of the greatest moments in your life, the ones when you felt heard and understood, when you knew you made a great impact in someone else's life.

What makes you happy and smile is a good indicator as well. Don't forget the difficult life situations that you handled well and learned from. Those are the moments you were operating from your core values.

Getting Rid of Your Saboteur

The answer is no. The saboteur will always be in you, and truth be told, the saboteur has a purpose. Its original function was to prevent us from doing irrational or dangerous things. Sometimes we need time to think things over before we make a good, solid decision or commitment.

When we commit to ourselves, we face the challenge of separating sabotaging thoughts from our true thoughts. The potential for inner conflict is created by our lack of accountability to ourselves, our insecurity about trusting our self, and the lack of immediate, concrete results from our actions and choices.

How to Deal with Your Saboteur in a Healthy Way

Here it is important to monitor the strength of your saboteur. When you set goals, your intention is to expand and to grow—anything involving change or growth upsets your saboteur and sets it into motion. Your saboteur will use the methods mentioned earlier to sabotage your intentions and your commitment, to yourself and others.

> Be aware:
> > Your saboteur changes over time because you change.
> > Don't argue with your saboteur, because you will not win.
> > Don't judge. Observe the type of thoughts you have or inner voice you hear, without attachment or judgment.

Step One:
Recognize the voice or thoughts of your saboteur. Learn to identify your self-sabotaging thought patterns. (See How Does Your Saboteur Take Centre Stage? section)

Step Two:
Give your saboteur the form you see it in - a witch, a judge, a bully, a monkey, a fantasy creature. Give it a name, a personality, and a life history.

To really connect to your saboteur, draw it and describe it in an essay. Answer the following questions about your saboteur:

What are its favorite things to say and do to you?
In what way does he find himself helpful?
Where does he get his information?

Write as much detail as you can. Though it may feel silly or dumb (saboteur words), this helps you place the saboteur outside of you.

Visualizing your saboteur as an external character makes it easier to observe your saboteur and notice more quickly when those sabotaging thoughts show up and hold you back.

Once you can visualize it and quickly identify the thoughts and presence of self-doubt, instead of being harmful, it can become useful. Give it a job like mowing the grass, getting firewood, brushing the cat, or whatever, to occupy it. By creating its life history, you will know what it likes to do. You create what works for you.

Your saboteur will be out of the way, allowing you to operate from your **I Am status** and make the best choices for you and the people around you.

Commitment to Others

Now that you understand the challenges in being committed to ourselves, it won't come as a surprise that being committed to somebody else can as challenging, if not more challenging.

Making a commitment to another person is difficult because you have to learn to make it an equal partnership. Now you are not only dealing with your own saboteur but also that of another person. When family members fight or friendships disintegrate, often present is one or both of the people's saboteurs.

Pause for a moment and closely observe the people in your life. What do you see?

When you look closely, you will see brilliant human beings who are dealing with fears, saboteurs, and insecurities operating from the only point of view they have of the world, just like you. We don't all see the world in the same way.

By not understanding where other people are coming from, we judge, dismiss, attack, criticize, argue, and use violence to persuade others that our view of the world is the right viewpoint. We continue to operate in this way in every situation and in every relationship we have from partners to family members, on all levels of politics, as long as it works. When it does not work, we often exit those relationships. It narrows our world to the few who agree with us.

How to Create Healthier Relationships

Do your best to walk in the other person's shoes when in disagreement. Try to see what the other person sees and feels.

When we do this, it becomes clear that we are all dealing with our own set of demons, insecurities and saboteurs. Relying on the expectations of good behavior and open-mindedness will always disappoint us because it is difficult to live up to those expectations, especially when we do not have the same expectations or know what are the other person's expectations.

Be honest - How often do you share your expectations in your relationships?

Sharing your expectations and asking somebody else what their expectations are is an ongoing conversation. But when we are aware of whom the other person truly is, what they expect and appreciate all they have to offer, we can commit to them and will have a higher success rate in creating a full and healthy relationships with them.

By using this approach, I can say I love my dad unconditionally. It took me a while, but I got there by really looking at all aspects of his life and seeing things from his perspective. I learned more about my grandparents because they were the key to understanding why my dad did the things he did.

Doing this gave me clarity about why my dad chooses to live a fear-based life led by his saboteur for over eighty years now. I know I will only be disappointed if I expect him to change. The only thing I can do is see his true self, even when the saboteur is talking, and set boundaries, so his saboteur can't hurt me and I don't give it any control over me.

Sometimes this approach can look uncaring, on the outside, but it is just the opposite. When we love someone so much, it is a challenge we face on constantly on special occasions or in daily interactions.

Commitment to others is especially difficult when your partner's strong saboteurs are victims, judges, bullies, or generals. Relationships that have weathered many challenges, like illness, stress or change, aren't always easy. But when we face difficulties together, supporting and encouraging each other 100%, no matter how much we may drive each other crazy, we see the depths of commitment and love in action.

When you are not committed to yourself, it will be difficult to commit to somebody else.

In a workshop I did recently one of the exercises was to make a list of all the important people in our lives, starting with the most important person. When we were done, almost nobody listed themselves. Is it because we take ourselves for granted or because we have a tendency to put others ahead of ourselves?

Commitment to a Cause

The last type of commitment is commitment to a cause, also referred to as goals. These commitments can be easier, if the stakes are high enough. The higher the stakes, the more commitment we give a cause.

Commitment to a cause is also more easily measured. You can follow the progress you make by achievements, progress and time. This applies to both personal and professional goals.

The following are examples of personal goals:

- ✓ Losing weight
- ✓ Quitting smoking

- ✓ Finding a partner
- ✓ Improving relationships with family and friends
- ✓ Balancing home and work
- ✓ Working on inner strength

Examples of professional goals include:

- ✓ Completing projects on time
- ✓ Finding the right career
- ✓ Balancing home and work

The more passion, confidence, courage, and willingness we invest in a specific goal, the more likely we are to keep our commitment and the more likely we are to succeed.

Reasons We Break Commitments

Often commitment has a negative association. This is the result of unclear communication in several regards:

- ✓ What the commitment all entails
- ✓ When the commitment ends
- ✓ Whether we can deliver on the expectations of others

These misunderstandings arise from assuming we know what we are getting ourselves into before discussing the facts. With this in mind the saboteur has a field day and will feed your fears so that your fears overrule your **I Am status**. And voila, the saboteur is back in charge.

Which fears will he use against us?

- ✓ Fear of failure (we don't like to fail or look like an idiot)
- ✓ Fear of getting hurt
- ✓ Fear of losing control
- ✓ Fear of change
- ✓ Fear of losing yourself

Everyone grapples with these fears and others. I've seen my clients, friends and family deal with all the fears mentioned above at some point in their life. Those that recognized their saboteur, named it and told it to get out of the way, pushed past what was holding them back. Others are still struggling, wondering why life is so hard.

The success rate of a commitment depends on if you made the commitment out of trust and understanding of what you were committing to or out of fear. When you truly commit out of trust and inner strength, you don't come up with excuses or blame others for setbacks. You are only interested in what the results of this commitment mean for you.

Interest or commitment!

Through unclear communication we confuse having an interest in something with committing to it. Having an interest is like having a hobby or being curious. An interest helps us learn and broaden our horizons. We only spend time and energy on a hobby or an interest when we feel like it or have extra time. The result is not intensely important to us.

The difference between an interest and a commitment lies in the result's importance. We may say that we are committed to someone or something but if we only invest a little time and have few expectations about the result, in reality we are still only in the interest stage.

By understanding all the elements of the five-point system - trust, conflict, accountability, commitment and the result, the easier you can make the distinction between an interest you have and the commitments you are willing to make.

Honoring a Commitment

The easy way to honor a commitment without any second thoughts is to make a commitment that feeds and is in line with the **I Am status.** You will be so passionate and fired up about your decision that it feels natural to follow through. It will not feel like a restraint or prison. You will want to be there and contribute to the world around you.

What is needed to honor a commitment is trust, clarity on what the commitment entails, personal responsibility, loyalty, and a connection to the result. We spend most of our time in fear regarding commitment, and forget to focus on the benefits commitment can bring. Commitment is an underutilized tool because our starting point is often feared, instead of love and courage.

Benefits of Commitment

- ✓ It opens up two-way communications between people.
- ✓ You can trust that you will get help when you need it.
- ✓ You have a support system (like a parent or a coach).
- ✓ You have somebody to whom to be accountable.
- ✓ You can give and receive guidance.
- ✓ You receive affirmations that you are important to somebody and are needed.
- ✓ You contribute to the human race.

Deep down, we all want those things. We all want to know that we are important to somebody and that we contribute to the world in some way. To achieve that, we need to master the art of being vulnerable, flexible, and adaptable, and we need to know how to ask for help.

Vulnerability

Vulnerability is often seen as a form of weakness. In reality, it is the highest form of strength and courage. Fears, like fear of commitment, do great damage to who we are, what we do, how we treat others and our **I Am status**.

> What does being vulnerable actually mean and look like in action?
> When you discover that you were wrong about something, you take full responsibility. You don't try to hide your mistake or blame somebody else. You deal with your fears and mistakes. Honesty is key.
> You have the courage to deal with difficult and delicate issues.

Most of us shy away from difficult issues or situations. We ignore them. When dealing with "the elephant in the room," you address the elephant (the issue), stick your neck out and show others your vulnerability and that you have nothing to fear. I admire people who do this, even when subconsciously I created the elephant, because I can't fix something if I'm not aware it's present.

You tell the truth in a kind way so that others can keep their dignity and self-worth. Being honest can mean that what you have to say could be painful for the other person. However, when a painful message is delivered in a kind, nonjudgmental, and compassionate way, people are more open to receiving what you have to say. The tips talked about in giving feedback in Chapter 4 are applicable when being honest and vulnerable.

You try to be your best self and do what you do best. Be authentic. People can feel when you are not authentic. We all want a connection with the real you, even when we are not aware what that is.

You ask a lot of questions, even when they sound dumb. Don't fall into the trap of making assumptions when you don't know something. Ask questions. When you ask questions, you engage with another person and make that person feel important to you. This is true for every situation. Consider how store clerks ask questions to serve you better (with the right body language, of course). How does that make you feel? Or how does it feel when you have a deep conversation with a friend, family member, or colleague, and they asks your opinion on a topic and listens in Level 3? Show your ignorance so you can attain the information you need.

You make bold suggestions when you are asked for advice or are in a brainstorming session, but you are not emotionally attached to your suggestions and do not worry what others will think of you. You just put it out there, and others can do what they want with it. Since you are not emotionally attached to the outcome, fear can't creep in. We want to be liked so much that we are inclined to tell people what they want to hear instead of what we really think, just because we are afraid to rock the boat or have people think badly of us.

You admit your weaknesses and limitations. It is powerful if you say, upfront, "Sorry, this is not my strongest area. Is there somebody else on this team who can do this better than I can?" If you bluff and say, "Sure, let me do this," and then screw up big time, people will doubt your commitment and honesty. In a good marriage, you often find that the partners complement each other's weaknesses. For example, if one partner is exploring their inner self, but the other is not, it might push the relationship outside of its comfort zone. If the love shared is unconditional, and the people involved are each other's anchors, they need to listen to each other. No matter the circumstances, the person you trust may see things you do not. Their insight needs to be recognized, not dismissed.

What do you gain by being vulnerable?

- ✓ People will trust you.
- ✓ When you are vulnerable, you show people the real you and don't play victim. You show your inner strength because you don't shy away from difficult situations, and you try to be as nonjudgmental and compassionate as you can about others and yourself.
- ✓ People know that they can trust you and that you are there to help them in the best way you can, even when you have to say a painful truth.

For example, we all have friends we trust to tell us the straight truth. When my children were teens, there times when we locked horns over issues. I would talk to certain friends, hoping they would side with me and say that I was right. Instead my good friends told me I was being old-fashioned and my kids were not the same as me. They advised me to let go and let my boys make their own mistakes. This made me look at the situation from a different perspective. I thank my friends for their honesty and vulnerability because those situations made me grow, sometimes reluctantly.

You are authentic and real.

When you are vulnerable, you are also transparent. People don't have to guess what you think or where you are coming from. There are no masks to hide behind and no games being played. When you know your strengths and weaknesses, you are more modest. You know what you can and cannot do. Knowing your strengths and weaknesses is Step One in the process of being true and vulnerable. When you start to know and handle them accordingly, you are on the right track.

- ✓ You have a strong connection to your I Am status.
- ✓ You operate from love not fear.
- ✓ You attract people who are loyal to you.

Another trait you enhance with vulnerability is honesty and loyalty. People recognize that you do what you say and say what you do. Trustworthy people will respect you for that, and if someone doesn't, you have to ask yourself if that person is worthy of your friendship. We all want loyal people around us, and one way to attract that is by being vulnerable.

Being vulnerable is not for the weak hearted. It is the opposite. When you have inner strength and stamina, you can show your vulnerability. We rarely teach our children this. Many of us still hide behind our masks and let our saboteur control how we present ourselves to the world.

We all want to be seen as competent and in control of our own lives. This sounds great, but most of the time we are not. We let our saboteurs and other people's opinions and belief systems control our lives. Nobody has the power to change somebody else, you allow others to change how you present yourself. Only you can change and you can be the change you want to see.

When you are vulnerable, in all its glory and strength, you give others permission to do the same. Some will rise to the challenge, and some will not. For the people who can't, I feel only compassion and kindness toward them, because they are prisoners of their pasts and their negative self-talk.

Do you ever tried to avoid certain people, who always talk negatively and have nothing nice to say?

I know I can't change them, but I can send love, even when I choose not to talk to them because I know they drag me down with them. Most of us avoid those mired in negativity. You just may not realize you are doing it. It's not that you don't like them but a conversation with them makes you feel tired and drained. I prefer to talk with people who challenge, uplift, or make me think because I feel interested in and connected to the person I'm having the conversation with.

As you've read in this chapter, there are factors that determine the quality of ingredients we use in our personal commitment glue. Some are easy to change, but for most of them we have to look deeper into ourselves to find the right strength for the commitments we value highest.

The more clarity we have on our reasons for and the importance of the commitments we make, the better we understand the need to create the results we want.

Consequences When Breaking a Commitment

What are the consequences of breaking a commitment? This is a loaded question.

We have many opinions and feelings about broken commitments. Breaking a commitment can trigger feelings of blame, shame, guilt, betrayal, and disloyalty. The emotions can come from the person who made the commitment, the one to whom the commitment was made, or both.

When a commitment to a cause is broken, the feelings we receive come from the people involved. One of the most common reactions is feelings of betrayal. The consequences of a broken commitment to a cause include dealing with different levels of emotions with the people involved and dealing with your own feelings at the same time.

In the previous chapters, we touched on the damage we do when we betray ourselves. With this in mind, it is of the highest importance that we understand and decide what commitments are important to us.

When we are clear on what commitments are important to us, we can act with integrity and honesty if we need to break a commitment or promise.

No one but you can determine when and what commitments are okay to break. You need to look inside yourself and do an internal check on your level of commitment, your **I Am status** and your emotional well-being.

Be honest with yourself - where are your thoughts coming from - your true self or your saboteur?

Try to find the voice of your true self. If you find that challenging, get some coaching sessions to find your true self.

If that suggestion brings to mind thoughts like, "Don't start thinking!" "That's too much work," "Where do I start?", "That's not for me," or "That's too much money" - Saboteur alert!

Just gently put your focus on the question - Is it in my best interests to find a coach to help me find my true inner self? When the answer is yes, you may only need six to ten sessions. You will find a lot of value in those six to ten sessions focused on finding your true level of commitment.

When we start being honest with ourselves, we may learn that a commitment we made is not serving the result we want. In the next chapter I will explain more about defining results for yourself in detail. The more you start trusting and leaning into your **I Am status**, the less you look for approval from others.

For most of the questions we ask ourselves during a day, we already know the answers when we are in tune with ourselves. When your inner self is involved in making a commitment, you will be more adamant and able to keep your commitments. If you have to later break that commitment, you will be more at peace with the decision and able to move on. It doesn't matter whether we choose to make or break a commitment, as long as our commitment is made with our **I Am status** and not by our fear-led saboteur.

As long as you communicate that with vulnerability and honesty, the people around you will respect your decision. Remember - only you know what is best for you.

Summary

- ✓ Commitment is the glue that bonds the building blocks of trust, accountability, and conflict.
- ✓ There are three different types of commitment: commitment to self, commitment to others, and commitment to causes.
- ✓ The difficulty of honoring a commitment to self lies in the fact we are only accountable to ourselves.
- ✓ When we break commitments to ourselves, we don't recognize the damage we do to our **I Am status**.
- ✓ When we betray our self, we stop trusting our inner guides, and our self-esteem plummets.
- ✓ Recognize who is influencing you: sabotaging thoughts or the **I Am status**.
- ✓ The saboteur uses a hard, demanding voice, with shoulds and have-tos.
- ✓ The **I Am status** has a soft, loving, flowing voice, with filled with the message - "Yes You can."
- ✓ Find out the details of your saboteur's image, history and triggers to create clarity.
- ✓ The saboteur likes to keep you in fear, and that fear will weaken the commitments you make.

- ✓ When your saboteur is talking to someone else's saboteur, it can be difficult to keep or agree to a commitment.
- ✓ If you have difficulties committing to yourself, you will have difficulties committing to another without feelings of self-betrayal.
- ✓ Committing to a cause is easier because the cause itself doesn't have emotions. Only the people involved in the cause do.
- ✓ You are the only one who can decide which commitments are important to you.
- ✓ The most powerful commitments you can make are the ones you make from your **Me Am status**
- ✓ Vulnerability is the highest form of strength and courage.
- ✓ People communicate more clearly, trust and are loyal to somebody who is vulnerable.
- ✓ In vulnerability lies the power of your **I Am status**.
- ✓ With vulnerability you operate from love not fear.
- ✓ When a commitment is broken, emotions like blame, shame, guilt, and betrayal dictate emotional responses.

CHAPTER 6

Result

With everything you think, say, and do, you create the life you live.

This is the truth. We may not choose the events or the environment of our lives, but we have the power over how we look at and deal with what happens on our life path.

Result can mean many things to many people. By examining the Canadian Oxford Dictionary definition of result as "consequences or outcome of something," and applying it as the fifth point in the five-point system for dealing with life, we will discuss the consequences of how we think, speak, and act.

Here are some everyday examples:

- ✓ You don't drink and drive, no matter how short the distance.

- ✓ Your children have a set bedtime with little wiggle room.
- ✓ You stretch the truth (cheat) on your tax return.
- ✓ You avoid conflict, at almost all costs.
- ✓ You have a strong opinion on society's hot topics, like teenage mothers, mixed relationships, the gay/lesbian community, politics,

The examples are endless. For now I'll focus on the above statements and backtrack to the root of those statements by dividing the statements into three categories of think, say, and do.

Think, Say and Do Chart

Think	Say	Do
Drinking and driving is not acceptable. or One or two drinks won't hurt.	I don't drink alcohol when I drive, because I don't want to be responsible if I get in an accident. or I will be fine with one or two drinks; they don't affect me.	You drink nonalcoholic beverages the whole time. or You drink alcohol.

Children need structure.	My children are at their best when they stick to a routine.	You put the kids to bed almost at the same time every night.
Everybody cheats on their taxes, and I will miss out if I don't.	Like everybody else I stretch the truth on my tax return. The government has money enough.	You cheat.
I don't know anything. / I'm not worthy. / I don't like violence. / They will be right. / I don't want a fight right now.	Yes, you are right. / We'll do it your way.	You give up without standing up for your beliefs and opinion, and therefore you put yourself down.
You will have thought about society's hot topics based on your beliefs, what you've been taught, and your life experiences.	This will depend on your beliefs, what you've been taught, and your life experiences.	You will defend your way of thinking at all cost.

Keep in mind this is a simplified think-say-do chart to show how our responses influence the results. Each category creates a result.

Go one step further: What are the building blocks of these three categories?

Think: What you think is everything you believe.

Your thoughts are influenced by things you've heard in life connected to an event (for example, you got a D on your report card, and your parent said you are dumb. You took that literally, and as a result, you believe you are dumb).

Your thoughts are also influenced by the media, what you experience in your intimate environment, and what you were exposed to when you were young.

Say: What you say is verbalization of what you think.

Often people don't stop and pay attention to their thoughts. You will notice that in what they say. Just listen carefully. Sometimes we are taught to say what others want to hear (being politically correct) and not necessary what our personal opinions are. The result is how what we say impacts us and others.

Do: Doing is the physical result of what you say and think.

Again there are two different ways of doing: physical actions and our body language. Conflict between our physical actions, what we say and our body language can create misunderstandings and mixed results.

The above is just the tip of the iceberg. In daily life these categories become confusing and difficult to dissect. Thoughts are complicated and it is hard to know which thoughts are true and which are false.

How the Saboteur Influences Our Actions

This is why it is so important to be able to recognize our saboteur. We need to know who is creating our thoughts - the **I Am status** or the saboteur. Your thoughts influence what you say and do.

When the saboteur is in charge, your sabotaging thoughts create inconsistency in what we think, say, and do.

Often we don't even realize it. When you really pay attention to what people say and do, you may notice that what they say and what they do are two different things. This is a good indication that this person is operating from their saboteur point of view. We all have periods when we are in the saboteur mindset.

My experience is that a large percentage of the population are not aware that there is an **I Am status** or a saboteur mindset Few people are able to see the difference in themselves or others. It is important to have patience with each other.

My philosophy is when somebody is inconsiderate or even means towards me, I know that they are probably coming from the saboteur mindset and not from their **I Am status**.

When you are in your **I Am status**, you can't hurt others. A simplified way to look at human relationships is to realize that when somebody hurts you, they will most likely be in the saboteur mindset.

Your best way to handle the hurt is to go into your **I Am status** for the strength to forgive and be grateful. This will help you feel safe and loved from the inside out, which is a most powerful feeling. Such an approach can be challenging. Only the strong and the courageous will do it, but it is worth the trouble.

When you come from your **I Am status** and the person you are communicating with is in the saboteur mindset, you can be true, genuine, and authentic, but if the other person doesn't or can't recognize it, there is not much you can do. If the other person is hurt, you might show compassion. You will do exactly what you need to do in that situation because your **I Am status** will never steer you wrong.

Goals

Results include our goals and what we want out of life, When asked what we want from life, our answers are often goals like the following:

- ✓ Good family life
- ✓ Lots of money
- ✓ Great friends
- ✓ Good health
- ✓ New house
- ✓ Great job

Write down your own wish list.

Now pause and really observe the way you think, speak, and act.

Are your actions helping you achieve your goals?

Good family

If you gossip or complain about family and friends, it is difficult to create a close bond with the people you love.

Lots of Money

When you want lots of money, what kind of steps are you willing to take to achieve that goal without hurting others? By others I mean everybody—your clients, co-workers, the environment and those you do not know but may be affected by your actions. Being dishonest, scamming people to get money hurts others. Everybody is connected to every transaction everybody makes. The more people who cheat on taxes, the more taxes go up. If the money stream was transparent, we would be shocked at where the money goes and how it affects all of us. Don't forget to ask yourself what you would spend the money on and how those purchases would affect those close to you, the environment and others.

Good Health

Good health is tricky one because it depends on our genetic structure, past practices, family histories of disease, stress levels and so many more factors. What we can control is what we eat and drink now and practicing healthy lifestyle habits. Be careful not to become judgmental of others who choose differently, because that influences how you think.

What is Your Vancouver?

The results we achieve are as complicated as our health and are affected and influenced by many people and life factors.

To simplify this convoluted concept, Let's imagine you live in Toronto and your goal is to go to Vancouver. If all your plans and decisions are leading you to Halifax, what are the chances that you will accomplish your life goal and end up in Vancouver?

The road from Toronto to Vancouver is not a straight line. You will encounter bends and hills to navigate, long stretches of prairie, possibly encounter dry spells, fire, floods or snow storms, closed roads, moose crossings, avalanches, mountains to cross, lakes to drive around, and many other challenges. If your goal is to accomplish this journey in a one day drive, you will be disappointed, because it is not possible.

Pursuing Your Goals

To learn how other people pursue their goals, I included the following question in my survey, "How do you pursuit your goals?" The most popular response was tied between "I make a plan and follow it with a sense of humor" and "I don't make a plan and I take opportunities as they come along" (both 38.1%). The next most popular answer was Other. After that

4.8% of respondents choose, "Goals, what goals. I have only dreams," and 2.4% (the lowest number) choose "I make a plan and follow the plan to the letter.

Q6: How do you pursue your goals?

I make a plan and follow the plan to the letter	2.4%	1
I make a plan and follow it with a sense of humor	38.1%	16
I don't make a plan and I take opportunities as they come along	38.1%	16
Goals, what goals I have only dreams	4.8%	2
Other	28.6%	12
		Answered question 42
		Skipped question 1

(Survey conducted courtesy of SurveyMonkey Inc.)[11]

"Other" responses.

1. I like to start with a plan, but always end up following where ever life takes me.
2. Focus on the top three main areas, then asses as I go along. I work with taking responsibility for my experience along the way.

---

[11] Ibid.

3. Love to plan, and then go with the flow as the unexpected turns in life are important to.
4. I make a plan and follow the plan according to (changing) circumstances. In other words. I will follow my plans, but not at the expense of everything.
5. I make a plan but it is a moving target with changes made along the way.
6. You have to roll with the punches. Things sometimes go wrong and you have to be able to smile and keep working through it to the end result that you are after.
7. I follow a plan. However, the plan may be adjusted as I proceed towards the goal.
8. I have plans, but not always follow them. I get lazy.
9. Try to make plans and if something else should arise that should be dealt with right away then the plans go by the way-side.
10. Yes, that sense of humor is necessary to help me maintain my sanity. I follow laws/governances that affect my plan, but makes allowances for any changes that may be necessary to allow me to continue to the ultimate goal.
11. I flip flop between the first three.
12. I make a plan but accept I don't have control over other people, unexpected events and circumstances ect.

Many of us try to plan and get mad or curse when things don't pan out the way we thought they would. From what I see around me, our society is based on instant gratifications. I want something, and
I want it now. This can be a new big house, a cup of coffee or perfect no-work-required health.

Sometimes we want things that conflict with one another, like good health. We want good health, but we also want to be able to eat anything we like in any quantity without gaining weight. We want all our electrical gadgets without facing the consequences of possible health risks or high hydro bills. The doctor might advise you to reduce stress and make a lifestyle change. This will require looking at your roadmap for life and asking yourself where you are heading. Typically, we are more willing to get a quick fix by taking pills than by changing our lifestyle.

Importance of Good Examples in Our Goals

We learn from everything that happens to us. In childhood we learn how to think for ourselves (when you are lucky) and what to take as our truth. People we know work for and admire, inspire us to mirror certain qualities and beliefs, like patience, stamina, and grace. The way others meet their life challenges give us courage and sets an example we may need to draw upon when faced with our life circumstances.

Encounters with health issues teach us how to respond to our body's needs and signals. Challenges with children and spouses teach us the importance of family. As our parents age, they set an example for how we do or do not want to grow older.

The lessons we absorb become part of our life plan and we need to ask ourselves constantly - Is this the road to our Vancouver?

Some of you believe you're better off without your family. You may be right. Some of you don't have family.

Our Family - Inherited and Chosen
Let's step back and clarify what family is.

While relatives, parents, siblings, uncles, aunts, cousins, are family, they are your birth family. Some people may not have family or are better off without them, but they have adults who take them under their wings, like my employers and friends, Will and Sue, foster parents, host families for exchange student, or somebody from Big Brothers and Sisters. They are your adopted family. As we become adults, we create families of choice from the friends we make and the communities we choose to participate in. The possibilities are endless.

My husband and I have been involved with an exchange program called Youth for

Understanding (YFU), a worldwide exchange program, since 2005.

The over a dozen young adults from all over the world that we have welcomed into our home opened my eyes to the influence of culture and the idea that the family we make through shared experiences are as important the family we are born into. When you or a student you are hosting experiences something life changing during your exchange, you either grow closer together or farther apart, like any family situation.

When I suffered a health issue while hosting two young ladies from Europe, their response and compassion to the challenges I faced made them family. While doctors tried to determine what was causing my frequent bouts of losing mobility, consciousness and energy, the girls stayed with us when they could have moved on. They helped with everything in the house from cooking and cleaning to keeping me company. From January until they left in July, they stayed with us, refusing to leave for a different host family. At

the end of their stay I was a little more mobile, and we took them to Northern Ontario for a weekend to show them more of Ontario.

After the illness and a risky successful surgery my symptoms eased and my health improved. I learned a huge life lesson. Their support for me is the definition of family - sticking together when the going gets tough.

You see people in the military and in first-responder units helping and looking out for each other. They refer to their units as their family. That makes a lot of sense because they see and do things together that they often don't share with other family members. In short, family comes in all shapes and sizes. There is no single definition of family. Your family is what you call family. It doesn't matter if you are blood-related or not. It is how you stick together, overcome hurdles, and be yourself without feeling judged. Families (born or chosen) are one of many influences that determine how we achieve the results we want in life.

How We Take Control of our Lives

We need to realize we have more control over our own lives than we think we do. It starts and ends with how we think, speak, and act. Our lives are arrangements of events. Some events occur daily.. Others are once-in-a-lifetime experiences, like winning a lottery. We experience momentary but influential events like an illness or raising children. From birth to death, our lives are in motion. Nothing stands still or stays the same. Every single event can be captured in a picture or a story. It is how you interpret the events that create us and the results we achieve.

I didn't ask to collapse or to have children who were sick or to be raised by parents who were in survival mode for years. Those were the cards I was dealt. What is mine is how I interpret them and what choices I make.

I could reject what happened to me and become resentful and bitter, or I examine the events, build myself life lessons and grow from them, turn them into compassion and gratitude.

I can clean out my backpack once in a while to make sure that my trip to Vancouver goes smoothly without excess emotional baggage, checking my course against my roadmap, which I have not lost but updated.

Out of sight is out of mind most of the time. If I do not ask myself what I want out of life, and what I have to do (my road) to get there, I will lose my way. We need to ask those questions of ourselves over and over again. When we keep asking these questions and are willing to be honest with ourselves, we will create the roadmap to our personal Vancouver. All our results in life come down to this. The results (or goals) in life are not about capital gain but about:

- ✓ Finding true happiness within ourselves,
- ✓ Finding our passion for life,
- ✓ Finding the courage to say, "Life is great even when it sucks."

Exercise Your Roadmap

Great people around us used this credo in their lives. It shows in their passion for their causes, like Dr. Martin Luther King Jr., Nelson Mandela, Gandhi, Mother Theresa, Shania Twain, or Will and Sue.

Be great, ordinary or in between, the results you achieve don't have to be written in the history books to be important. What matters most is what you find important and what mark you want to have on the people around you.

Try writing your own obituary. Write down how do you want to be remembered when you pass away That is your Vancouver.

Now look around you and ask yourself, am I on the right road to get there? If so, please keep going and enjoy the journey.

If not, it is never too late to switch directions. Remember that life is about the journey, not the destination. Create compassion and gratitude for your life, and your return will be above your expectations.

But first, we have to acknowledge and become aware of where we are and where we want to go. By recognizing, accepting and admitting the truth of an event, deed, action, we acknowledge its existence. An acknowledgment is a thing given or done in return for a service. Acknowledging our past, the people, deeds and events of our lives is so important if we want to move forward, especially if we hold the following important three things in mind: thought, speech, and action.

We know that we all want to been seen, heard, and understood. Do you acknowledge all the aspects of your life? Not only the good, wonderful things, but also your skeletons in the closet and your deepest fear? How can we acknowledge somebody else completely when we push away part of ourselves?

Facing Our Challenges

To achieve results, we need the face the challenges in our relationships with each other and with ourselves. By asking the question, "What is the biggest challenge you face in any relationship?" in the questionnaire included in Appendix C, I learned some of the challenges we face on our road to results.

Most respondents believe that "Not to take everything so personally," (42.9%) is the biggest challenge they face, followed by "Staying calm when I'm under pressure (28.6%), "To listen and to feel listened to," (23.8%) and "Dealing with conflict," (19%).

Q4: What is the biggest challenge you face in any relationship?

To listen and to feel listened to	23.8%	10
Dealing with conflict	19.0%	8
Staying calm when I'm under pressure	28.6%	12
Not to take everything so personally	42.9%	18
Other	14.3%	6
		Answered question 42
		skipped question 1

(Survey conducted courtesy of SurveyMonkey Inc.)[12]

"Other" responses:

1. Feeling like you are being heard. I can listen to people when they need to rid their story, but often when I need to do the same I feel that the other person just wants to get it out so we can go back to talking about them. This doesn't count all the time thought.
2. To handle criticism.

---

[12] Ibid.

3. It is hard to ensure that others truly understand what I am communicating.
4. No general challenges.
5. Different relationships, different challenges.
6. Some or all above can be present during a conflict, depending on my/their personal situation at the time. If one or both of us is pre-occupied with other stresses at that point in time, the conflict may escalate much faster than if there is no other stress involved.

We all want to be heard, as I've said many times. Almost a quarter of the people surveyed doesn't feel heard and have difficulties with listening.

Do You Feel Heard?

The question now is what came first, the chicken or the egg? Do we ignore what others say because we don't feel listened to or are others not listening to us because they don't feel heard by us? The only way to solve this conundrum is to really practice the three levels of listening described in Chapter 1.

When we feel ignored, we have to remind ourselves that we don't know what's going on in other people's minds. When we think nobody is hearing us, we stop hearing others. This leads to depressing thoughts, feeling invisible and feeling unacknowledged.

When we stop and acknowledge feeling of invisibility, we can move forward into thinking more clearly and create a bigger, different perspective about what is really happening at that moment.

When I feel ignored, after acknowledging how I feel and listening at Level 2 or 3, I often discover it was my own mindset that made feel me feel invisible, not something somebody else did or said.

Sources of Inner Conflict

Dealing with conflict" is a skill you can learn. Sadly, many of us haven't learned to do that effectively. You pick up most of your conflict resolution skills in your home from your parents and siblings as you grow up.

When we take everything so personally, we are not alone. Most of the population does this to a certain degree. By instinct we carry around every experience we have and relate experience we hear about from others back to ourselves. That is how we instinctively assess if a situation is safe or hostile. It also informs our view on the world in which we function and the roles and behaviors that are expected from us in society.

To a degree, we learn this as a child. The moment our children are born we have a hard time saying no to them, so what do we teach them? They learn, "That everything in life is about me, because if Mom or Dad can't say no to me, then I'm special and above others. I get what I want without earning it."

The result is children who never learn how to think for themselves. And when we're old enough to live on our own, we're still attached to what our parents told us because they never taught us to think for ourselves and be independent.

As a result, we create a society that practices a conditional dependence on love, freedom, and acceptance. This leads us to question if it is acceptable to take what we discover on our own as as our truth, or not? We fight with ourselves over basic truths.

If we take the experiences of family and others as part of our truth but don't feel it is truth, we betray ourselves. If we don't take what others tell us true as our truth, we betray our parents, friends, and others.

We are between a rock and a hard place. Most of us will choose to betray ourselves to create the illusion of peace. What we forget is that resentment and frustration bubble up beneath the illusion, like a volcano that is sleeping but still boiling. The pressure builds to a point that it boils over, and all hell breaks loose.

Self-Examination

The next couple of chapters cover how we can get the results we want without hurting people around us. But first we have to be ready, willing, and able to see when and where we neglect to acknowledge our life, our challenges and our goals.

How can we expect to change anything if we don't know what we need to change? It is easier to complain about the people around us and make them wrong than to really look at ourselves. Such an approach delivers only short-term gratification with a hollow, empty echo.

Since I started to look at my thinking pattern and watch what I say and do, I've almost banished the empty feeling. It returns when I slip into the old habit of taking everything personally.

By acknowledging that I sometimes fall back into my old thinking pattern, I find it much easier to get out of that empty mindset. Sometimes this process takes just minutes and sometimes it takes days. Both are neither good nor bad. They just are.

The power lies in getting out of the mindset. The trick is to not beat myself up and avoid it in the first place. I need to have compassion for myself as I have compassion for others who slip and fall.

We are our own worst critics. We view ourselves differently from how others see us. That's why I love feedback on my behavior, as long as it is given in a loving, constructive way. When I become aware of how others see me, then I have the chance to choose what to do.

I consider, "Are they right? Will tweaking my behavior improve the relationship?" If so, it is to everybody's benefit that I change. When I can't see the benefit, I'm less willing to change.

Don't forget that every time you consider changing, your saboteur will be sitting in the front row telling you what you need to do and think. Not only do you have to find out for yourself if this other person is right, but you also have to figure out which thoughts to follow. Is it your saboteur addressing the feedback or your loving true self? With practice you will get it the hang of it.

Understanding Feedback

Start by not taking everything personally. Remember that often what others say or give feedback on has more to do with them than with you.

When we give feedback or comment on another person, we tell our point of view. The unspoken implication we think, is that if they don't take our feedback as truth, we will believe they are dumb, not worthy to be our friend, or included in society.

We often mirror our deepest fears in the feedback and comments we give to others. We want to be seen as smart, capable, and professional. We feel that we need to convince the others that our view is right, and we will do everything to achieve that, even if that means rejecting their opinions and ideas.

I believe it is very important how people deliver feedback so both parties understand what is truly being said. When I'm giving feedback, I always do my best to do it with compassion. My Vancouver is to empower people to be the best they can be. To do that I learn right beside the people I teach. There is so much to learn about great communication. Different events in life require different communication tools and skills. It is often hard to detect when you're doing it right. Even when it is done "right," will the other see it as right too?

Communication is a two-way street.

Somebody starts the conversation, and then it depends on how the other person receives the message. You can deliver a message with the best intentions, but the receiver might have talked to a person before you and gotten chewed out. They will then be less open and listening on Level 1, 2 or 3 to what you have to say. Often you can see how your message is received by the other's facial expression and how they respond. Sometimes you get a mask and have no clue how your message was received. You may get a confirmation and agreement with what you've said, but later find out that they never agreed with you.

You can only do your best. Your best will vary from day to day because different events influence your mindset for the day. When you are a confident person, you will react differently to situations than when you are feeling insecure.

Dealing With Bullies

A bully is not a confident person. Bullies mask their insecurity by steamrollering others. When we keep this in mind, we have a better chance of changing the bully culture in schools and the workplace. We should focus on empowering people instead of pointing out what they do wrong. That doesn't mean that we stop addressing undesirable behavior. We help them see their strengths and their personal greatness so that they don't need to bully to feel secure.

The more confidence we have, the less we have to hide behind our masks of insecurity. Let's be honest, most of us have been both bully and victim at one point in our lives. The thing to do now is be gentle with ourselves and learn from our mistakes. Teach ourselves and our children that failure and making mistakes are great learning tools. Without them you don't know when you are doing things right.

Asking for Help

How can you figure out what you want, when you don't know what you don't want? How do you know when it is light outside when you don't know what darkness looks like? This book is designed to empower people and give them the power to start thinking clearly. However, this is not a substitute for professional mental-health support if that is what you need.

And please, when you do need help, ask for it. Don't be proud or stubborn. I recommend finding a therapist you trust and who is on the same wavelength as you. They can help you to move out of the mindset that doesn't serve you. I hope and pray that all of you find the courage to create the life you want and use all the building blocks that are handed to you, including the good and the bad.

Summary

- ✓ With everything we think, say, and do we create the lives we live.
- ✓ The thoughts we have come from our beliefs, repeated sentences we've heard, and things connected to our life events. Speech is the verbal expression of what we think.
- ✓ There are two different types of action: physical action and body language.
- ✓ Our thoughts, speech, and actions create our results in life.
- ✓ Become aware of what you want out of life.
- ✓ What is your Vancouver?
- ✓ Be impeccable with what you say.
- ✓ Don't take everything personally.
- ✓ Don't assume anything.
- ✓ Always do the best you can every single day to keep your Vancouver in mind.

CHAPTER 7

Family Cultures

To discuss family culture, we have to start at the beginning with the explanation of the five-point system as a whole—what it does and where it came from. I created some graphs to give you a visual concept of the system. All the five points are intertwined and connected. We have to work with all of them if we want to get the most out of life.

For example, you need accountability to handle conflict in a healthy way, and you need commitment to trust. Without trust, accountability, healthy conflict, and commitment you may end up with a result you don't really desire.

When you look at the graph below, you get a simple visual about how complex our relationships start out.

Diagram: A pentagon labeled "I AM STATUS" at the center, surrounded by five pentagons labeled **Trust**, **Conflict**, **Accountability**, **Commitment**, and **Result**, with arrows pointing inward and between them.

From the moment we are born, we experience life as in this graph. Parents and caretakers all over the world teach the principles of this graph from their perspective. When every aspect of the graph is in strong working order, we will experience those great feelings of confidence and accomplishment. We remember these feelings as happy or proud moments. We feel peaceful and connected at these times. We've all experienced moments when the graph worked this seemingly magical way.

However, life changes and pushes us out of our comfort zones. The challenge is to remember the graph and to use all five points in a confident way that allows us to grow mentally and emotionally.

The moment fear steps in, the five points will be off balance. We know when we have a broken bone we need to see a doctor, otherwise we will be in pain for the rest of our lives when using the broken area of our body. The same counts for our emotional state. When one pillar has a fear base belief (broken bone), like a lack of healthy conflict resolution skills, the rest will be compromised, and it will be difficult to maneuver through life. Every challenge we encounter will throw us off. Luckily that doesn't always means that we have to see a psychologist or that there is something wrong with us. Most of the time our willingness to look and change our thinking patterns is enough.

The graph below shows what happens when you place insecurity or fear in the spot for accountability.

The system is still doing the same thing, but instead of drawing on your accountability abilities, you are now drawing on insecurities. The origin of insecurities is fear - fear of not being enough, fear of losing a loved one, fear of embarrassment, fear of losing status, or maybe all the above. Needless to say, the moment happens to our system, our saboteur takes control.

As discussed in Chapter 4 our saboteur is our counterbalance and is connected to our fears and insecurities. Let's not fool ourselves and think this only happens when we are adults. This process begins when we are babies. That is why the first seven years of life are so important. The impressions we gather in that time become truths in our belief system. When we never question our beliefs or expand them, we do ourselves a disservice.

Living an unexamined life, will not help you achieve the results (goals) you desire, creating disappointment, even resentment toward life itself. To keep your Vancouver in sight, it is important that you check your five-point system on a regular basis. When you grow and change, so does your five-point system. You need to check what mindset you need to achieve your goals. It is important to see where your insecurities are located.

When I examine my view on money, I review:

> Accountability: I know where my money is and where it is going.
> Commitment: I don't spend more than I can and am happy with what I have.
> Conflict: I deal with money problems right away so that I can keep the damage as small as possible.
> Trust/insecurity - This is my biggest challenge. My truth was that when I had to deal with money I would assume a mindset of scarcity. When this saboteur (fear) was in control, I didn't trust my judgment. The fears of losing face, embarrassment, and even losing our home and business dominated my thinking. It resulted in a perceived scarcity of money.
> Result - In the end, my mind created the viewpoint I was looking for, and that was scarcity.
> Take Your Fears to the "Therapist's Couch"

To understand your fears and how they are holding you back, you may need to take them to a relationship therapist to examine both sides of the fear. This exercise involves using your imagination, not making a real appointment. Start by getting a pen and paper and making yourself comfortable.

Start writing what bothers you about your fear - be it your relationship with money, health, education, and so on.

Then switch sides and let your fear "talk" Write down what your fear has to say about its relationship with you.

When you look at what you wrote, you will see what you can work on to conquer your fear. I did this to look at my fear about money. Below is what I wrote in my "session" with money.

Relationship therapy:

I'm sitting on the couch at the relationship therapist with money next to me. We know we have some issues we have to work through before we can move forward in our relationship.

I get to go first to tell the therapist about our relationship. I look at money, then the therapist, and I start.

"I'm very unsure about money, and that makes me nervous. I never know if or when he will show up. Or when he will show up, is he there 100 percent? I never know. There is a lot going on in money that doesn't seem transparent for me. This gives me a feeling that he's hiding something from me. How can I rely on somebody when I feel I don't get his 100 percent attention? Also my parents are not happy with him. They find him lacking. Their point of view has a big impact on our relationship, especially when money does just the bare minimum. I don't want a divorce, but I want more out of our relationship. I want to be free with money in a way that will serve us both the most. I'd like to travel together and fix up the house and help the children to achieve their dreams and goals. Nothing earth-shattering, just a comfortable life with appreciation from money for what I do businesswise.

Now it is money's turn.

I'm not happy with her either. Every time I show up I feel that I'm lacking something. When I'm generous, she is happy and content, but when I have to scale down, she goes into fear mode and tunes me out. I have no way to reach her. I know where she gets it from. It is the same pattern I see at her parents' place. They are still afraid of me. Our happiest moments are when she is connected to the mindset of her in-laws. Then I feel appreciated, worthwhile, and always enough. But to be honest, why do I want to be with somebody who doesn't want to be with me? That is the impression I get. I get it that it can look like I'm not transparent, but hello, where is the trust? Is that not the main ingredient for a great relationship? Ellen is right; I don't want a divorce either. I hope and pray that she can let go of her fear so that we can have an open conversation about how to best serve each other. Her goals are great, and that is absolutely something I can do while being transparent. We both have to stop listening to commercials because they give a wrong impression of me.

Game plan:

We will start trusting in each other and stop listening to others who think they know better about what my relationship with money should look like, because they make everything cloudy. We will celebrate the victories we achieve and support each other when there are hiccups. We will realize that every relationship has its ups and downs. And nevertheless I am willing to have a great, trusting relationship with money.

You can put any topic on the therapist couch. You can dissect your fear the same way I did my money fear. Just do the graph in the way I did.

Using the Five-Point System Graphs

Take a mindset that cripples you and fill out the graph. Your fear and insecurity goes in the circle that is accurate for you, and find out which areas of your life are affected by that mindset.

If I put my relationship with my parents in one of points, (it doesn't matter what subject you choose) the circle will always complete its cycle. The circle in itself is simple to understand, but that doesn't mean that it's always easy to detect what cripples us, because we know what we know.

Luckily life has a way of teaching us. It gives us clues about where we can look for growth and where to expand emotionally, mentally, and even spiritually. Our job is to look and discover.

Our bodies give off clues about where we have to look but most of us ignore all the signs, and that gets us in trouble repeatedly. By running away or putting our heads in the sand we make it more difficult to deal with the life events we don't necessarily have control over. We may not have control over lots of things in life, like losing a job, getting an illness, being hit by a car, and so on. We can always choose how we handle situations. When an unexpected event happens, we are thrown off our game and off balance, and we may panic. This is a natural reaction.

When our five-point system is solidly in place, the panicky feeling will fade after a while. This means we will still feel other emotions like anger and sadness, but we are calm enough to think clearly.

When one of our five points is dominated by fear or insecurities, it can take longer or be almost impossible to think clearly because the fear is in control. Let's take a look at the graph below that depicts when the outside environment comes into our inner environment.

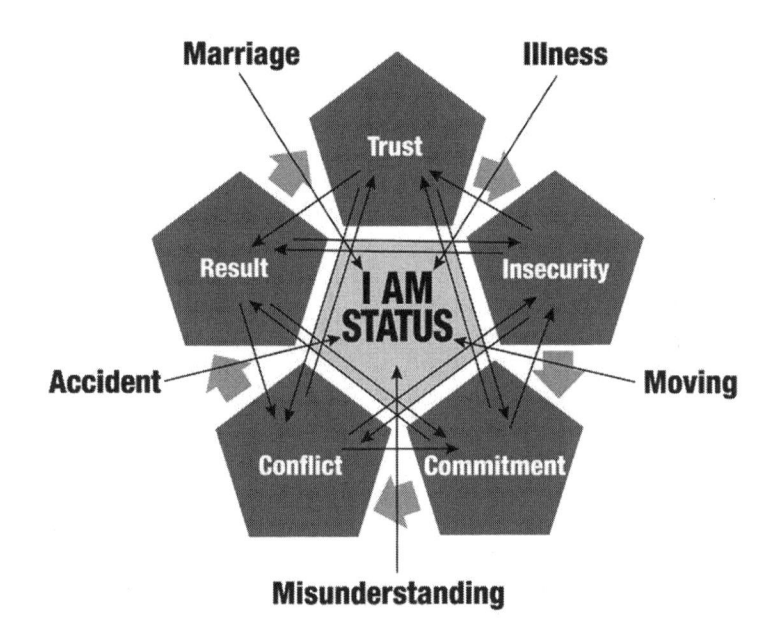

Diagram: A central pentagon labeled "I AM STATUS" surrounded by pentagons labeled Trust, Insecurity, Commitment, Conflict, and Result. External arrows point inward from: Marriage, Illness, Moving, Misunderstanding, and Accident.

As you can see, life gets more complicated. Life can resemble a knotted ball of yarn. All the yarn is there, but we don't know where the beginning or the end is. We only know that we can't use the yarn the way it is now to make a beautiful sweater.

It is no wonder that we have difficulty seeing clearly when fear is involved. As I discussed before, we all have insecurities, and we picked up most of them by the time we were seven years old. There will be fears we develop later, but fear related to life experiences are normally easier for us to pinpoint. We know where they came from. They're like big red flags. It could include a fear of dogs after being bitten or fear of romantic relationships after you were abused in one. We can see where these fears come from. You still need courage to conquer these fears, but the outside world understands what you are facing and is generally more willing to help you. It is easier for us too because now we can blame somebody or something else without questioning our beliefs.

The difficulties with the fears we get before we are seven are so subtle and ingrained that we don't even recognize them as fears.

Questioning Our Truths

When we take something on as our truth, it becomes part of our belief system, and we function through our beliefs. Everything we think, say, and do stem from our beliefs. Nothing can be more frightening than to ask yourself, "Is what I believe true? Were my parent's right when they taught me this belief? Is my society right to believe this? Is my religion right in their teachings?

To make it more visual, see the graph below. When you put a light-yellow color in the circle of your home environment that is where you grew up. You absorbed the beliefs in this space and took them as truths. This is understandable. it was all we saw, experienced, and had around us. It is like air. We know that air is all around us, but it is hard to see. How can we expect to react differently to an event in life when we don't recognize the options other perspectives to the same event can give us?

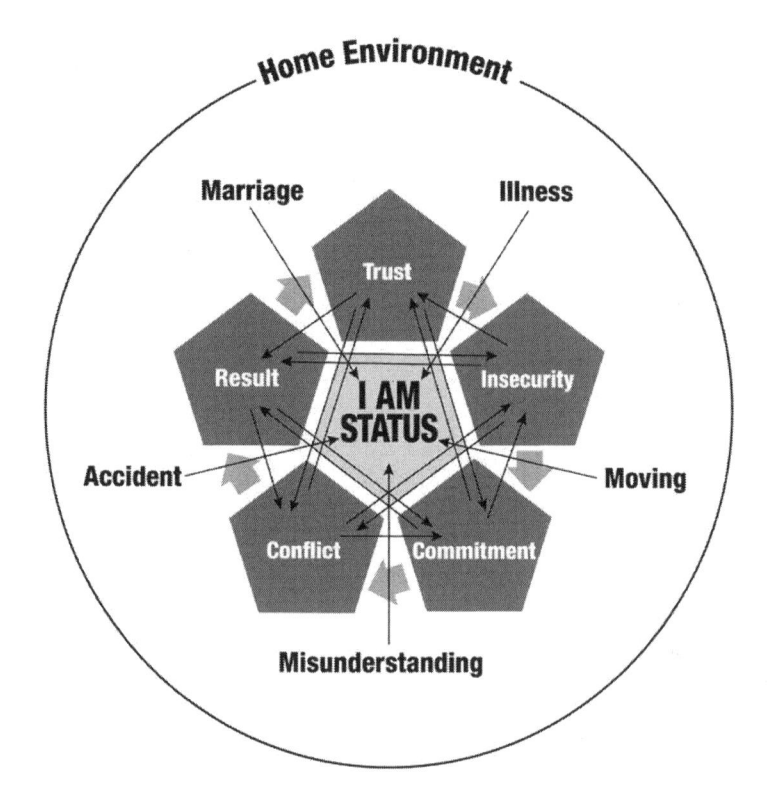

Home Environment

- Marriage
- Illness
- Trust
- Result
- I AM STATUS
- Insecurity
- Accident
- Moving
- Conflict
- Commitment
- Misunderstanding

I'm not saying we have the right to blame our parents for everything that is not working in our lives. That would be the easy way out and unfair to them because they were raised on a similar graph, only their yellow was a different yellow. Different generation, time frame, and other variables, but the same graph.

This covers our children too. We raise them from our beliefs and life experiences. My conclusion is therefore that we often copy the beliefs and insecurities from our adult role models and apply them in our own lives. It is up to the individual to find out what is true for him or her.

The greatest gift we can give our children is to teach them to think for themselves. Don't take what everybody else says as the only way to go. It would be great if the school systems taught this as well, but unfortunately it doesn't. For example, history is taught by learning about historical events, but the story comes only from the perspective of who's telling it. The English version of coming into Canada and its settlement is very different from the natives' perspective. They both believe their version is true and they are both right. When you look at it from all angles, all versions can be true. It is a matter of how you look at it. This counts for everything that has happened in the past and for what is happening right this moment and all over the world.

When you have a disagreement with somebody, you will defend your point to the end because you are right and the other is wrong, you believe it is as simple as that! This mindset is transferred through multiple generations, and if we don't break this cycle, we will transfer it to the next generations.

Is this the most beneficial attitude to attain the results in life that we desire? What is the legacy we want to leave behind for our children?

If we don't change anything about the way we are doing things now, we all can agree that we will have a hard time ending up in our Vancouver. By just looking at the graphs we can see how easily we can get sidetracked and wrapped up in insecurities and fear.

Finding Our Gems

The most fearful thought of all - we are transferring our fears and insecurities to new vulnerable generations without even being aware of it. The only way we can stop that is to start looking at our beliefs in a loving, compassionate way.

To stop the downward spiral of transferring our insecurities we have to start taking responsibility, see the previous graph and really encourage others to think for themselves. Each and every one of us has a lot to offer. We are all great in our own way. You may know the saying "Nobody is perfect." I say everybody is perfect in his or her own way.

From my relationships over the years I've learned I may not like a person or agree with him or her. I may not be friends or may not want to be interacting with somebody, and I may not understand where the other comes from. But I've never met somebody who had nothing to offer and who didn't have one great asset to draw from. We all have hidden gems in our makeup. I tell you each and every one of us possesses an impressive list of gems in our personalities.

Our **I am status** is beneath and between the five-point system and the belief system. It is basically the invisible glue that gives us strength in life. When we face challenges, we automatically turn to our strengths. This happens subconsciously, so it is hard to see that we do that and what our strengths are. I find myself leaning on humor and gracefulness when I'm dealing with illness, and I use persistency to get the medical help I need.

In young children it is easy to see their strengths. We all have heard a mother say what her child is good at or how he or she responds to the world. That is their **I Am status**.

When I look at my two grandsons, I smile. Even at two and a half years and ten months old you can see differences in their personalities. They are both wonderful but different. The oldest one is resourceful, generous, and creative, and the younger one is humorous, decisive, and bold.

For now you can't see clearly yet what insecurities they have picked up. They will be more visible later. Now they are still operating from their **I Am status**. The older we get, the more we get buried in the beliefs we take on and the more insecurities we create. There is a saying that drunks and children always tell the truth. Most of the times this is true, and do you know why? The barricades fall away for the drunk and the children don't have barricades yet, just their **I Am status**.

We all have moments when we operate from our **I Am status** state of mind. This is important to remember because this awareness will be your fuel of hope. Hope that we can be a better person, hope that we can achieve our goals and dreams, hope that we can change our bad habits, and even hope that the world becomes a safer and more peaceful place. The more you connect to your **I Am status**, the more you trust yourself and create compassion for others.

I used to work with convicted underage kids. People asked me many times how I could go into the correction center and interact with inmates. My answer was always the same: when I see the youth, I look at what is in them (their **I Am status**) and I try to show it to them to show them they are worthy just by being themselves and that they don't need masks to protect themselves from their insecurities. All of them were great guys who had bad habits. With some luck, some education and a lot of work on their own, they can change their habits. Even if we helped only one or two young men find their way back to which they've always been, we did our work well. Every person counts, but not all of them could see how great they actually were.

Masks We Wear

Many of us are lost in the five-point system and use masks to camouflage our insecurities and hide from out fears. Behind those masks we feel miserable, misunderstood, unworthy, and conflicted. The best weapon we have to defend ourselves is to be vulnerable with ourselves and toward others and to find our own gems in the **I Am status** state of mind.

This is what I want you to take away with you, after you finish this book - **All of us are remarkable in our own way, and that includes you.** Start believing that you are worthy of what life has to offer and that challenges are there to make you grow and not to punish you. You have plenty to offer the people around you. We all need each other's **I Am status** to find out who we are and who we want to be.

I love my parents for all that they've shown me about how I want to live my life. Other people's examples can inspire you or show you what you don't want. Instead of viewing something negatively (what we are inclined to do), we can choose to view the same event as an opportunity to learn.

Again, how can we know success if we haven't experienced failure?

How do we know what will work if we haven't seen something that doesn't? I am thankful for all the examples people give me, the good and the bad, what to do and what not to do. Everything is a learning tool that I can use for my journey to Vancouver.

The more we are clear about our **I Am status** the more we will take of our masks off and live a freer life.

Summary

- ✓ The make-up of our personal five-point system is a mixture of the interpretation of the system from both our parents.
- ✓ Parents transfer their insecurities to their children.
- ✓ To reach your Vancouver you have to question your beliefs.
- ✓ Taking your fears to an imaginary relationship therapist is a way to discover how to sidestep your fears.
- ✓ We may not always be in control of what is happening to us, but we are in control of how we react to it.
- ✓ We often copy the beliefs and insecurities we see in our adult role models and apply them to our own lives.
- ✓ The **I am status** gives us strength and backbone in our lives.
- ✓ Everybody is unique because every **I am status** is unique.
- ✓ Insecurity in the five-point system creates the masks we hide behind.
- ✓ By observing or experiencing what we don't want, we can embrace what we do want by understanding the difference.

CHAPTER 8

Societal Cultures

The other layer to the five-point system is the layer of your societal culture. This particular layer is located in between the light-yellow area and will add texture to the graphs in Chapter 7.

Imagine that every culture has a different color, and imagine what it would look like when you mixed different cultures in with the color you give your society. Some shades would be so close together that you hardly see a difference, and other shades would create totally different colors when mixed with yours.

If you grew up in country blue, you will have different societal influences than country red. See the graph below for a representation of where we live. Metaphorically it's like fish in a fish tank. For the fish, the tank is their world. It's the same for humans.

Our societal culture is our world. We play, work, stress, and love within this culture. Children are raised with the cultures they live in even if we don't realize it.

Society Culture

According to Webster's New World Dictionary, the definition of culture is "improvement of the mind and manners: civilizing tradition like folklore, folkways, education, arts, costumes, instruction, architecture, habit, study, inheritance, family." This definition includes many different topics that will be hard to define. Take folklore or habit or inheritance—we can't take a picture of those that will explain what they actually are, not like a picture of a building that explains the architecture of a country. So as you can see, societal culture is something almost immeasurable and hard to pinpoint.

The only way you can understand it is by experiencing it.

I will not go into the history of cultures, just because there are books written on this subject by people who have deeply studied societal culture and have a better understanding of it.

I want to gently observe the differences in people with the five-point system in mind. Let's dive into the ripple effect of our cultures.

Mixing Family and Societal Cultures

To start, every family has its own culture. In this space you know what is acceptable and what is not and what is expected from you. This is your base reference. Everything you encounter in life will be measured by the standards you know. Everybody in your color area understands the dynamics of this culture. This area will be affected when a new family member arrives, and adjustments are needed.

You can see that clearly when a baby or even a baby pet enters the household. Those are the easiest adjustments, believe it or not, because the newcomer comes in with an open mind and ready to adapt to the environment. Their reference includes only the five-point system and their **I Am status,** without any insecurities and old beliefs. We accumulate those from the first culture we encounter by taking in insecurities from those who raise us.

When a new member arrives, like an older new pet, a new parent, partners of the children, a sibling, or somebody from a different country, it is more challenging. Now we not only start mixing different shades of your color but different colors from multiple people, along with different insecurities as well. People only really know what they have seen, heard, tasted, smelled, touched, and gained through proprioception ("one's own," "individual," and "perception" - It is the sense of the relative position of neighboring parts of the body and the strength of being employed in movement).

What is Culture?

If a person who spent his whole life in the interior of Africa. He knows all the ins and outs of living in the Savannah.

He knows what is expected of him, the dangers and the opportunities that are present in his environment. This is his light-yellow area and is very clear to him. Now this man travels to Toronto, Canada. What new experiences and thoughts will he have?

- ✓ It's cold.
- ✓ Do I have to eat that?
- ✓ How do you travel here?
- ✓ How do you find your way around-which way is south, north, east or west?

- ✓ Everything looks so different.
- ✓ What are the bathroom rituals?
- ✓ Can you use endless amounts of water?
- ✓ The roads and the amount of people are so confusing.

Those are just some of the thoughts he may have.

For a person who's lived his whole life in Toronto, these thoughts and questions may seem silly, because they are familiar with the landscape, the customs and the expectations. But put them in Africa and their thoughts will be very similar.

How can we know something if we have no experience with it? This is what culture is —you can't see or touch it; you only can experience it. Yet we judge others when they are confronted with something new.

How often do we judge others, not realizing that we're doing so? It all comes down to the fact that we see everything from our point of view and so it can be difficult to adapt to a different perspective. Immigrants from all over the world will tell you that it is not always easy to move to a different country, especially when they expect that they can work the same way in a new country as the one they left. This is a form of close-mindedness that we don't recognize in ourselves. We need change or others to point it out to us.

In life we learn first our family culture, and later on when we go to school and engage in other activities outside the home, we get more exposed to societal culture.

We learn more about world culture, depending on which color country we live in and how much we travel.

Media Culture

With the Internet and computer savvy young children, we have to watch out that the Internet and computer games don't take over the raising of our children. TV and the media, in all its forms, is part of our societal culture.

That is a scary thought because there are a lot of mixed messages on the Internet and the media. The Internet and media can be considered an independent world culture in itself, and often driven by money and opinion, not by truth.

I feel empathy for young parents these days because they encounter challenges that I didn't have to deal with. When I look at my son Adrian and my grandsons, I already can see it. Mr. Two-and-a-Half-Year-Old is quicker on a cell phone than I am. He doesn't even talk much yet, but boy, does he know where to go if he wants to play a game on an iPhone. He is one of many children of his generation who are computer savvy before they can talk. Is this by definition bad? No, we simply have to keep in mind what our rewards/

goals are regarding our children? As you can see in the graph below, we are get information from all different sources.

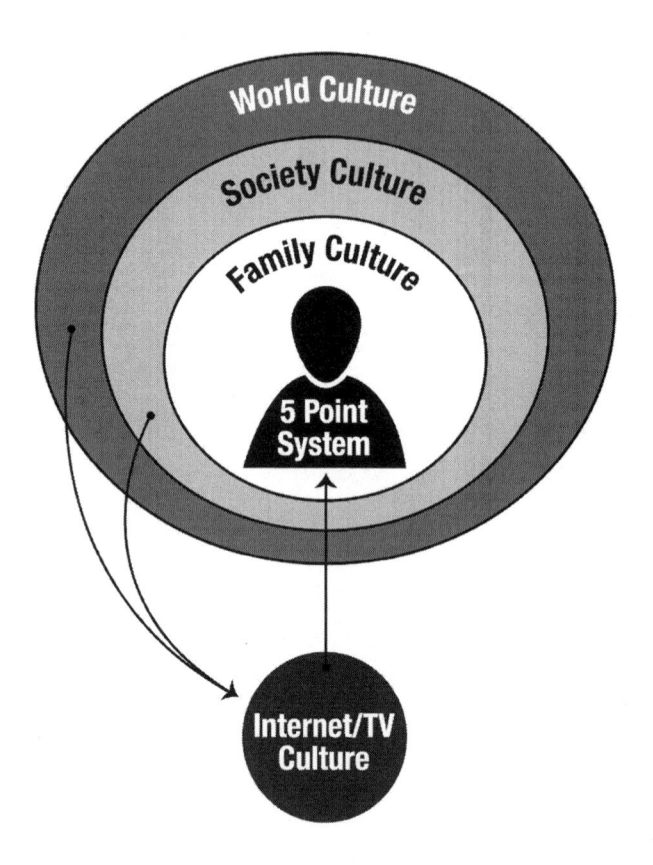

Diagram: concentric circles labeled "World Culture", "Society Culture", "Family Culture" surrounding a figure marked "5 Point System", with an "Internet/TV Culture" circle connected by arrows.

Internet and TV beliefs are created by the societal and world cultures and feed the five-point system (you). It is up to you to figure out what is true and what is not. Are they of service of you, or will those beliefs hinder you from finding your rewards? That is the question!

Influence of Cultural Differences

Sometimes it is hard to grasp cultural issues and differences, as I have seen firsthand with our exchange students. My involvement with the Youth for Understanding exchange program included helping as an area rep with arrival orientation when the students first arrive in Canada. They are still thinking with their own cultural point of view (they know what they know).

It's noticeable that students from the same country have a differing societal culture viewpoints, depending on their geographical locations. With students from border countries, you start seeing different cultural views and customs. They may come from the same area in the world, but there are differences.

At the arrival orientation it is not unusual to have over twenty students from all over the world: Finland to New Zealand to Chile and everywhere in between. They reflect the cultural traits from their piece of the world. What is normal for one is unknown or taboo for another.

We hosted a young lady from Australia, and she arrived in January. It was winter in Canada and summer in Australia. She asked if the trees were sick because they had no leaves. After our explanation that all trees shed their leaves in the winter and will get new ones in the spring, we found out that in her area of Australia (the Gold Coast) most trees keep their leaves year-round. This was something we didn't know and found very interesting.

Another example is bathroom etiquette. This may make you raise your eyebrows, but there are different ways of dealing with bathroom use. Students who travel from Canada to Japan get an education in Japanese bathroom etiquette before they go so they can transfer into the Japanese culture more smoothly.

In European countries like the Netherlands, Belgium, Germany, France, Denmark, Austria, and Switzerland, the people may look the same and dress the same, but they all react differently according to their culture because that is what they know. With a large percentage of North America's ancestry being European you would expect that we share the same customs and beliefs. However, over the centuries North America has developed its own culture by adapting to the landscape and the different cultures combined within it.

Wherever we go and whatever we do, we not only draw on our knowledge from our family culture but also from our societal culture. This may sound great, but it has a downside. With all the information we are exposed to from the moment we are born, it gets harder and harder to see our own five-point system and our **I Am status.** These core parts of who we are get buried under the family and society's cultures.

It leads to many of us dealing with the demon of indecision and doubt. In the education system and in the home we teach from societal and world culture viewpoints. In the family we teach the family's culture. None of this education deals with recognizing and empowering our **I Am status**. We teach from the outside in, with the assumption that children are blank slates. As a result our **I Am status** is infused with the pressure of collective insecurities.

Earlier in the book I mentioned how difficult it is to raise children to their full wonderful selves. Now you know why that is - because to do that parents have to let go of everything they have been taught by their parents and just focus on what this particular child needs. The uniqueness and potential of each child needs to be respected by not just the parents but also the education systems and society.

One Set of Rules for Everyone?

One set of rules for everyone seems to be a logical and realistic expectation for any society. Without such universal laws, we imagine a world in crisis where people will kill each other, there will be no boundaries and utter chaos.

Have you seen the news lately? Are we really further ahead with our one-size-fits-all rules? Chaos still reigns, killings still happen but what about our emotional and mental development? How far have they advanced?

I have my doubts. As a society we haven't focused on how great and significant our **I Am status** is. So what would happen if we focused on raising our children to their **I Am status** and helping adults find their **I Am status** instead of following what the society expects? That is the big question, and here is the answer.

People will start trusting in themselves and finding value in their existence. We won't have to pretend that we are better than we feel we are, because we can draw more freely on our own inner strength and knowledge.

By getting lighter ourselves, we will become lighter with others and nonjudgmental.

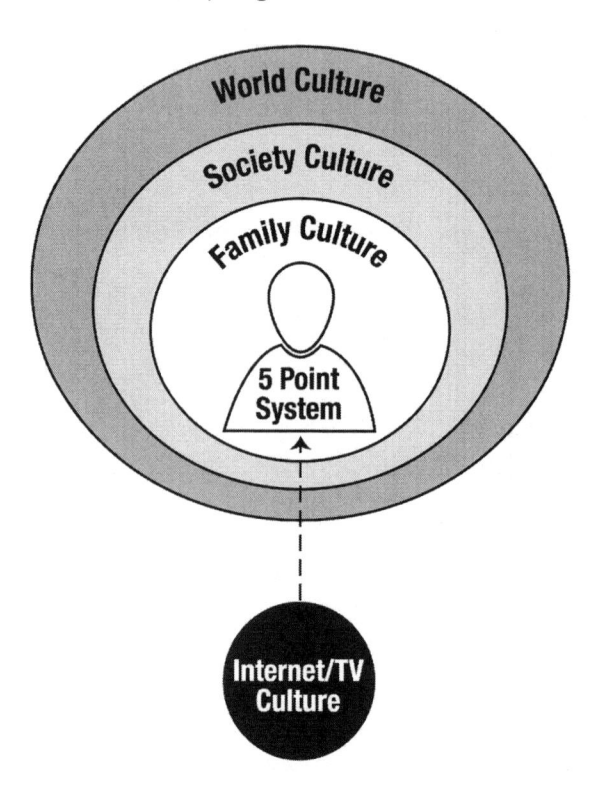

See the difference between the graphs when we teach from the inside out? The graphs are the same, but the colors are lighter, and that represents our state of mind. The more transparent our **I am status** is, the clearer and more genuine our communication with others.

Does that mean that everything we learn from family and society is wrong and we should dismiss it? No, that is not what I am saying. We just can't be attached to what we teach our children. We need to be okay with them making choices that we do not always understand and even go outside what is normal.

Basically, we need to teach them the five-point system and their **I Am status.** When we draw on a healthy five-point system and **I Am status**, we do what is best for ourselves and for the people around us. I have seen this demonstrated repeatedly with people like Will and Sue, Nelson Mandela, Mother Theresa, my husband's grandfather on his father's side, and my father-in-law.

All the great names in history, from Jesus, Buddha, Abraham Lincoln to Dr. Martin Luther King Jr. knew the secret of the five-point system and possessed a strong **I Am status.** There were times when they were unsure or questioned what they were doing but what kept them going was that they were more afraid to betray themselves than face any punishment they might receive from society. They were aware what the consequences were if they did betray themselves.

Commitment to Self Rewards

Most of us don't pay attention. We betray ourselves much easier and more often.

Questioning life itself is diving headfirst into the previous graph, and that means unraveling our beliefs, which will awaken the collective insecurity system of our family and societal cultures. So the "easy" way is to go with the flow, follow in the footsteps of your family and society, and not rock the boat, but there's really nothing easy about it.

By following in others' footsteps and taking on their truth as the absolute truth, we betray our own values over and over again to the point we forget who we really are. This creates resentment, and empowers fears.

Looking at your beliefs takes courage and is not for the faint of heart, because you not only question your own beliefs but those of your family and culture. It is quite an undertaking, and your path is not always clear, nor the rewards known. But I promise you the more you look at your **I Am status**, the greater the reward is. Rewards come not in the form of more money, a better job, great health, a higher status in the community, or a faster car. The rewards you will receive won't necessarily be linked to status and prestige. That reward system is what we learn from family and societal perspectives.

The following are the rewards that you will receive:

- ✓ Gain confidence
- ✓ See different perspectives, opportunities, and options
- ✓ Reduce anxiety and stress
- ✓ Worry less about end results
- ✓ Be more open-minded
- ✓ Improve relationships
- ✓ Feel happier
- ✓ Live life the way you want
- ✓ Be nonjudgmental

And the paradox of all this is when we have all the above, we will have better health, can change to a job that we are passionate about, possibly make more money and attain a higher community status. We will also notice that we assign a different level of importance to those things then we did before.

Creatures of Habit

Fear of change stops us from trying to unravel our beliefs, Most of us are so afraid of change that we are upset by the smallest changes.

Have you ever had your routine interrupted?

How did that make you feel?

Were you off for the rest of the day, or did you recover quickly and move on?

I bet if you work in an office and have staff meetings regularly that you instinctively sit in or close to the same spot every time. You probably have daily routines. Most humans are creatures of habit.

Animals are creatures of habits as well, only they are not attached to their routines to the degree humans are. I have learned some amazing things from animals about letting go.

My three dogs, Pasha, BA, and Angel taught me about letting go. When BA was hit by a car he had to have surgery and stay at the vet's overnight. He was in critical condition and we didn't know if he was going to make it. When I came home, Pasha and Angel were both unsettled. The next day he hadn't improved. When I came home, Pasha and Angel were still unsettled. On the third day, I got the call that BA had passed away. I wanted to bury BA at home, so we went to the vet's and brought him home. When we drove in the laneway, Pasha and Angel came flying up the laneway and jumped into the truck. They sniffed BA. When they jumped out, they were calm and happy again. Knowing what had happened to BA was enough to settle them and allow them to carry on. They changed from nervous, agitated, and unsure to accepting and calm.

I believe the reason they adjusted so quickly was because they were less attached to the outcome. They took life as it came.

But I have also noticed, the more domesticated the creature, the more they are attached to life they have—humans, dogs, cats, and working animals. Domestic animals may be more in tune with the human energy fields and feel our agitation. They take that on as truth.

We as humans can learn a lot about adapting to change from the animal world. Some societies' cultures are more advanced in this area. The native tribes from all over the world from the Amazonians, the aboriginals, Native Americans to the African tribes are closer to nature than the rest of us and are used to adapting to new environments and events.

The only thing we have control over is how we react to a situation, "to change the world, start with yourself." This may sounds cheesy and over the top, but it is so true, and it is the only way the world ever will see peace.

Look at Graph 3 again more closely. Can you see the ripple effect? Whatever we put in the middle is what moves outward. When the **I Am status** is light, it will filter out into the world. The more light people we have, the lighter our family and societal cultures are. By lighter I mean populated by people who are open-minded, nonjudgmental, and confident and who see lots of different perspectives and options.

The outer rings are a reflection of the state of mind of a collective group of middle rings, which combine to become family and societal culture.

I'd like to share some famous quotes about change for you to ponder.

> Everyone thinks of changing the world, but no one thinks of changing ourselves.
> —Leo Tolstoy

> The world as we have created it is a process of our thinking. It cannot be changed without changing our thinking.
> —Albert Einstein

> Change your thoughts and you change your world.
> —Norman Vincent Peale

> We are taught you must blame your father, your sisters, your brothers, the school, and the teachers but never blame yourself. It's never your fault. But it is always your fault,

because if you wanted to change, you're the one who has got to change.
—Katharine Hepburn, Me: Stories of My Life

Here is to the crazy ones. The misfits. The rebels. The troublemakers. The round pegs in the square hole. The ones who see things differently. They are not fond of rules. And they have no respect for the status quo. You can quote them, disagree with them, glorify or vilify them. About the only thing you can't do is ignore them. Because they change things. They push the human race forward. And while some may see them as the crazy ones, we see genius. Because the people who are crazy enough to think they can change the world are the once who do.
—Apple computers Inc.

Coping with Change

As inspiring and true as these quotes may be, what makes it so hard to embrace change in our lives? Back to our fear again. When we encounter a change, our brains go into overdrive to sort out if we are in danger. All kinds of alarm bells go off, and we have to sift through which ones are valid and which ones are not. See graph below.

CHANGE

Beliefs
Habits
Expectations
Chance Of Failure

Over our lifetimes we create a sort of library of coping mechanisms that we rely on when we encounter change. All those strategies fall under the umbrella of either beliefs, habits, expectations, or failure, and therefore they are challenging to change. It doesn't help either that we view change as an automatic negative, with ideas of what something should look like (what will society say if it is different?).

When we experience a change, our brains go to our libraries to find out the best way to deal with the situation. If our libraries are never updated with new books, we will reread the old ones, and never expand our horizons. Therefore we always keep change at arm's length, which makes us inflexible and inadaptable. You have to ask yourself - what is more difficult, questioning your beliefs, habits, and expectations or continuing to follow the same path you're on and just existing instead of truly living?

One of the reasons I've included my life path in this book is to show you that change is possible with great rewards, greater than you can imagine. The moment I read the quote from Apple I smiled because

I have felt every emotion and am familiar with every description they came up with. The great news is I've learned to connect with people in all walks of life, and I try walking in their shoes. This makes it easier to be nonjudgmental and not judging gives me freedom to be free of drama in my life. Does that mean that nothing startles or affects me, that negative events just wash off me, and that nothing bad ever happens again?

No, life is still throwing me curve balls. You recover quicker from your "bad" experiences. You don't have to stew with no way out in a particular situation. I not only learned to love and honor my own **I Am status** but also everybody else's even when I don't understand the things they do. I'm still working hard to let go of the concept of what something should look like. But hey, life is a journey not a destination, and my life goal is to enjoy the journey.

That is actually my wish for you too. We are alive now, in this moment, so let's make it worthwhile and enjoyable in the time we have. To do this we have to start at the bottom, and that is trusting our inner wisdom. If we don't do that, then our foundation will crack, and everything on top will crumble. Every home improvement show will tell you that. In the next chapter I will explain step by step what you can do to build a great life on top of a solid foundation.

Summary

- ✓ You only know what a societal culture is by experiencing it.
- ✓ Things we know we have experienced.
- ✓ Our experience with our family and societal cultures will form the base of the way we view life.
- ✓ We always compare other cultures with the first culture we became familiar with.
- ✓ When we don't understand something, we are inclined to judge it and be closed off to other possibilities.

- ✓ We get information on how to live and what is important from family, societal, world, and media cultures.
- ✓ With all the information we surround ourselves with, it is more difficult to find our **I Am status.**
- ✓ We have been teaching our children from the outside in. The **I Am status** is therefore buried under unimportant societal rules that zap the energy and life out of people.
- ✓ Teach children from the inside out; make every **I Am status** front and center. This will make every culture stronger and nonjudgmental in the long run.
- ✓ Take with you the beliefs that strengthen your **I Am status**, and push away the ones that hinder you and take you down.
- ✓ The big impediment keeping us from looking inward is the fear of change.
- ✓ We have to let go of our coping mechanisms when we encounter change.
- ✓ When you let go of fear, the rewards will exceed your expectations.

CHAPTER 9

Love

The most potent glue in life is love. Yet this is another greatly misunderstood concept. The Webster New World dictionary defines love as "strong affection or liking for someone or something" or "a passionate affection of one person to another." So what does that actually tell us? For me personally, nothing.

Love is an emotion with many different angles and is easy to misinterpret. I want to point this out to you because it is of great importance for our journeys on change. Without the reassurance (glue) of love, changing something can be impossible.

Let's be clear on something upfront. We can't change somebody else even if we want to. And let me tell you, over the years I have tried to change Luke, but it never worked. However, with me showing him that change is not always a bad thing, he was more willing to follow my example in his own way. This works the other way around as well.

The concept of love is as complicated as the concept of fear, with the same number of faces and sometimes with the same difficulty to visualize. Love is as simple as fear. It's almost always hiding in the background.

When we stumble upon change in our lives, both our love and fears step forward. That is when we choose which one we are going to rely on. With change connected to danger, we are more inclined to go into fear mode. This judgment is made in a millisecond.

Trusting in Love

What would happen if we started trusting in love more? I don't necessarily mean romantic love. I am talking about human interaction love.

For example, a couple of years ago I drove through Detroit, Michigan, after the car industry had closed down, and by accident I went off the main highway into one of the Detroit neighborhoods and got lost. To get back on track, I needed directions. I stopped at a gas station that had steel bars for the windows. My immediate thoughts were fear-based and filled with what could go wrong.

Then I stopped myself and thought, "Ellen, you go in there, and you ask politely for directions. They will help you, and all will be fine." So I went in, and five people came up to me to find out what I wanted. When I explained that I was lost, they were more than willing to help me and gave me clear directions.

I picked this scenario because it had everything going for it to keep me stuck in the fear perspective. I had fearful thoughts of violence, discrimination, assumptions based on media reports, and perceived negative assessment of my situation, all in a couple of seconds. It took me longer, to calm myself, and become open asking for the directions I needed. I had to switch from fear to love. In fear mode, I wasn't in any shape to receive information because I was all in my head and not open to outside influences. By switching to love, I opened up for clear communication with other humans.So for me there is more to love then what is described in the dictionary.

Romantic Love

Almost everywhere we look we are confronted with images of romantic love. It sometimes appears as if romantic love is all that love is.

We, as a society, romanticize love to a degree that if it is not of the romantic kind, we may dismiss the feeling of love and fall back into the fear mode. If you want to know what romantic love is, just look at the dictionary. When we talk about romantic love, we may say we feel butterflies in our stomach, warm tingles, and happiness. When we imagine it visually, we perceive it as a couple holding hands, kissing all the time, Harlequin Romance books, and love story movies with happy endings. We show romantic love by giving gifts, physical touch, doing things for each other, and saying I love you. This all sounds great, doesn't it? We all recognize and want this version because we are taught this is what love is.

Even in relationships with others like parents, siblings, children, animals, nature, or objects, we demonstrate these feelings and behaviors. It may look different than standard romantic

love, but the core is the same. Looking at a baby will give most of us a warm fuzzy feeling, and walking your dog makes you happy. It's the same with hanging out with friends and having good conversations with parents and siblings.

That's what I'm talking about when I talk about the romanticized love umbrella. See the graph. If our feelings don't fall under the romantic heading, we dismiss them as not a feeling of love, because how can something be love if we don't get the expected feelings?

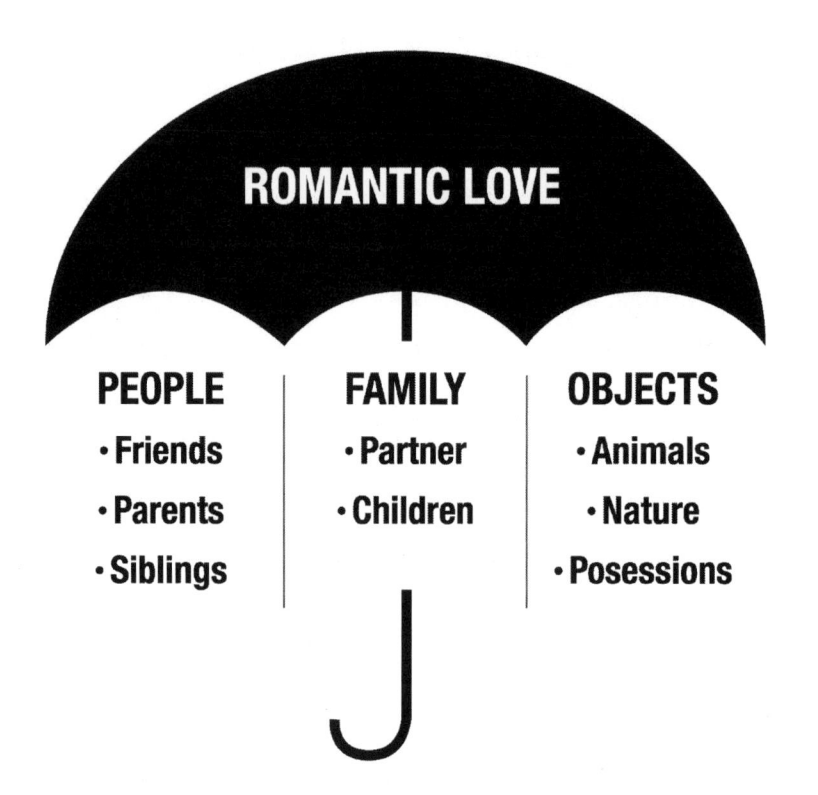

```
                    ROMANTIC LOVE

    PEOPLE          FAMILY          OBJECTS
    • Friends       • Partner       • Animals
    • Parents       • Children      • Nature
    • Siblings                      • Posessions
```

This makes our view of love very narrow. On first sight this might not be bad, but what happens when life events occur? Is romantic love flexible enough to bend with changes? The moment something happens our brains search our personal libraries for solutions to the event, based on past experiences. It then connects emotions to the event. This all takes place on the subconscious level, within our personal five-point system. That's why people can react differently to the same event. It also makes us afraid of change, because the moment something changes we have to re-evaluate our feelings of love.

When we connect our perception of love to somebody or something else, if that somebody or something changes, so does the feeling of love. This way love comes from the outside into us. Take a look at the graph again. If you take away, say, family, there will be a hole in the love experience. The same thing happens if you take away people or objects. It is not surprising that we view love in this way, because this is what family and societal cultures teach us.

Now we come to the stickiest part on our journey. We already unraveled the impact of the five-point system, family and societal cultures, and the media culture on our **I Am status**. Now it is time to understand why we let all those insecurities stick to us.

Conditional Love

It is as simple as conditional love and as difficult as the human race teaching conditional love as the only true love there is. I'm talking about the human race as a whole.

I came to this conclusion by observing human interaction. If you don't dress, talk, walk, and so on, in a certain way, we take our love away. It's not verbalized that simply, that's why it is difficult to recognize the love game we are playing, but we are playing it nevertheless.

Instead of saying we take our love away, we make the other person feel guilty, ashamed, unworthy, not one of us or wrong. We do whatever we need to do to make the other person feel small and unimportant until they do what we want because if the person does the "right" thing, then he or she deserves our love.

Here are some examples:
- ✓ Good girls are home before one in the morning.
- ✓ Making love when you are not married is sinful.
- ✓ It is not appropriate to wear that (however "that" is defined where you live).
- ✓ My parents and brothers play the guilt and shame card on my sister and me. We both immigrated to new countries, and as our parents age, they need more help. That is the daughters' duty not the sons' (from their perspective). Other examples of when we use the withdrawal of love (acceptance) to reinforce family/societal values:
- ✓ Not having a Christmas gathering with the family, like in the movies, is wrong.
- ✓ Not having turkey for Christmas dinner is wrong.
- ✓ Children have to contact their elderly parents at least once a week - that is their duty.

- ✓ I must have an engagement ring after two years of dating; if not, does he really love me?
- ✓ The man has to make the marriage proposal.
- ✓ At the wedding we have to invite the "right" people, and it has to look a certain way in conjunction with cultural traditions and the latest fads.
- ✓ Children can never have a tantrum. If they do, you are a bad parent.
- ✓ Children can't share their opinions; if they do, they are undisciplined.
- ✓ Not taking your parents' advice is practically a sin.

These are little things that we learned from our family and societal cultures that have enormous consequences on our lives. We frown upon something that is weird or different for us personally because we don't understand the other person's perspective. This is especially true among family members or partners. With children we explain it as generational differences, but among people in the same age group we are quicker to judge.

The way we judge depends on where and how much insecurity sits on our five-point system. The more insecure you are, the more you judge and the more difficulties you have with change in general. To keep life as controlled as you can, you want to keep your love under control as well. For you to give love, you want the security of receiving love in return, but only in a way you can understand and therefore feel.

But everybody gives and receives love in different ways. Assumption is a big cause of misunderstanding love. Over the day we are bombarded with information about whom and what to love from the media - the perfect cars, food, finances, and cosmetic products to the perfect mate. If you don't act right now, you miss out on all the great things in life, and maybe you won't get accepted by <u>the</u> group.

Humans are herd animals, and our basic instincts tell us that acceptance in a group is crucial for survival. So the underlying fear is that of being an outcast, which in primitive times could mean death. Over the centuries we have refined the expectations we have about how to behave, and again this behavior depends on your societal culture.

Take the differences I've noticed between The Netherlands and Canada when it comes to weddings, for example. Now mind you, what I know about weddings in The Netherlands stems from the time that my age group got married. I expect it is probably different now.

In The Netherlands a proposal and expensive engagement ring were not a big deal. Often a couple started talking about marriage after being in a relationship for a couple of years. The planning of the wedding day was done when you had the venue, invitations, flowers, cars, clothing, guest list, and a priest or minister. If you had a bridesmaid, then it was a little girl and a little boy as ring bearer. My wedding was planned in approximately a month.

There were no bridesmaids or groomsmen and no theme or color scheme. My wedding dress was secondhand because I found it unnecessary to spend a huge amount of money on a dress that I would wear once. My wedding ring was the same one as my engagement ring.

We followed some local customs, like the neighbor drove us everywhere that day from church to the reception hall and home afterward. That was it.

In Canada it seems to be all about the proposal and the engagement ring. If that is not done right, you are questioned about whether he really loves you. I'm not sure how quickly engagements are formed, but dating for a while means a ring with a wedding date set, because a ring without a wedding date is weird. Then you have to have a wedding theme and color scheme. The perfect cake and food is a must.

To find a wedding gown you need all your friends and female family members. You can't get married without bridesmaids and groomsmen —the more the merrier. You can't disappoint anybody, so who do you choose? Planning a wedding takes at least a year, otherwise are you doing it right? Can you think of somebody who had an unconventional wedding and the reactions they had to deal with? It is all about meeting other peoples' expectations and whether it is done "properly."

My experience with Canadian weddings seemed to revolve around the bride and everything being perfect. The bride's families seemed stressed while the groom's families were hardly involved?

Marriage is a union between two people, not one. What I see is that the moment an engagement is announced, all the conversation and relationship energy becomes focused around the wedding day, and not much is left over for discussing life after the big day.

Often after the honeymoon a couple is lost because they forgot to connect with each other in the last year when they were planning the wedding. Maybe they never talked about some important life issues like handling finances, wanting children or not, getting to know the in-laws and setting future goals. These life questions are important for the survival and thriving of the relationship that a marriage celebrates.

I'm not against wedding days with all the bells and whistles. But I believe is that the couple getting married should enjoy the process of creating the wedding day of their dreams, not what is expected from them by family, friends and society. They need to talk to each other about life questions and continue getting to know each other.

Clear Expectations

Having expectations limits us in our relationships with others. Take a minute to imagine a life without trying to live up to others' expectations.

Ask yourself, how much do you have to offer the world that is hidden behind the different masks we use when we pretend in order to meet other people or society's expectations. How freeing would that be?

If you had no expectation defining you, you could choose any career you wanted (within your capacity and circumstance), and you wouldn't expect anything from others. We not only carry others' expectations of us, but we carry around our expectations of others.

As we get older, we carry more expectations of us. Some elderly people smarten up, and those are the ones who do their own thing and live to the beat of their own drum. When a young person does that, we call them a rebel. Look again at the quote from Apple. They call those people geniuses.

I can hear questions rising about how the world can function without rules and expectations. In the ideal utopian world, everybody lives with no expectations.

Weddings are just one example of the expectations we have in life. We could talk about the dream job, the perfect family, having perfect health, and even when and how many children you want to have. It all boils down to expectations. The more clarity, courage, compassion, and honesty we have regarding our own wants and needs, the better we can communicate them to others.

If you come from love when you are communicating precisely about what you want, it is then up to the other person how they react. That is not your responsibility. It is not something you can control.

Like many people who choose to leave their country and move to another one, when my husband and I decided to immigrate to Canada, our parents and relatives weren't happy.

We involved them as much as we could as we set up our new life. We went with my father-in-law to Ontario to look at farms, but we were clear on what we wanted. We didn't take on our parents' feelings and expectations as our own. Had we done that, we would still be living in The Netherlands, and lost our clear **I Am status**. People who try so hard to live up to others' expectations, lose sight of whom they are. They become a player in their own life instead of the producer.

Life controls you instead of you controlling your life, if you lose sight of who you are. At that stage family, societal, and media cultures orchestrates your life. We get buried under the outside information that comes our way.

We find it hard to figure out who we truly are, and if we change the status quo, our saboteur comes in and starts trying to destroy our desire to change.

Power of Unconditional Love
Is there a solution to all of this? Yes there is.

By shifting from conditional love to unconditional love we expand our vocabulary and understanding. When we expand our vocabulary and understanding in words and actions of love, being truer to our **I Am status** is easier to do, and life events become less of a burden. We find more joy and happiness.

Conditional love leads to many subliminal expectations and conditions. The media portrays this as true love. Our society and family romanticize love creating a need for others' approval to feel special.

Unconditional love is the most mystical and forgiving love of all. I can tell you from personal experience this is the most incredible gift you can get and give. It is so special that the feeling alone can make you cry with joy. It would surprise me if you haven't experienced it yourself at least once.

Would you be aware if this type of love was given to you? Just sit with this question for a moment before you answer too quickly.

Our brains automatically start searching for an answer to this question as we read it. If we haven't filled in our brain library with the feeling and understanding of unconditional love, we won't find it. Therefore, we have to involve our hearts and bodies, as well as our brain when answering this question.

It is like putting an advanced computer program on a computer that operates on Windows 98. Everybody will tell you it won't work. The program and the computer can't "talk" together.

This is happens to us as well, when we listen only to the head and not to the heart and body. Sometimes our **I Am status** has been buried under all the other influences since birth and we can hardly find them.

I Am Status & Unconditional Love

We know what we know (this is our personal computer program). With us not being fully in touch with our **I Am status,** we start to live in a fantasy world. Like in the movies, it looks real, and to a certain extent it makes sense. But you are playing somebody else's role. It is not truly you.

The reason I'm so excited about our **I Am status** is because they are beyond amazing, all of them. To describe an **I Am status** I have to use a metaphor.

When you look up on a clear night and look at all the stars twinkling with a full moon you can almost touch, everything is clear and at peace. Slowly you let your eyes pass over the sky, and you feel small and magnificent at the same time. When you gently focus on different stars, and you see how brightly they shine. You see which ones are closer, and try to find the Big or Little Dippers. You are in awe of the unbelievable panorama you have the privilege to experience. It is a miracle, pure and endless, and you take it all into your being (body and heart). You feel you are in the sky like a shiny star, and the only things you see are other shining stars. All is well in the universe. You realize you are one of the shining stars.

That is what the **I Am status** looks like without conditional love, and outside influences. You may think this is too good to be true, but I promise you it is not. That galaxy lives inside each and every one of us. You can't exist without it. In the next chapter I will explain how you can access your **I Am status,** if you want to.

Accessing Unconditional Love

For now I want to focus on the magnitude of real love, love that is deep, forgiving, compassionate, nonjudgmental, and free of expectations.

The **I Am status** is one way to access love, and can be mostly felt in with one's heart. To fully express and experience real love we have to get our bodies involved.

Your body gives off clues about what it needs and how it feels every minute of the day. Our bodies are so smart that they will tell us (with gut feelings) when something is wrong. When we see or hear something that makes us sad, our bodies will tighten, and a sad emotion will follow. Basically it is first a physical reaction, followed by an emotional reaction. Most of us never learned to pay attention to the messages that our bodies give us.

To become more attuned to your body, make time each day to just sit for a moment, slowly and fully breathing in and out, and focus on what is going on inside of you. You will be amazed at how much information you perceive. It takes practice, but persist. Widening your ability to get in touch with your body and emotions as well as your mind, gives you a strong range of information to access when trying to understand yourself and your place in the world.

I was scheduled to go to a conference, and a couple of days before I was due to leave, I noticed that my body didn't want to go. It was telling me "I need rest". We're going on a trip next week already."

However, I still planned to go. The night before I had to leave, I got the stomach flu, and couldn't go. I spent all the time scheduled for the conference at home in bed. My body was smarter than my head. I didn't want to listen, so my body made sure they had to listen.

This kind of scenario happens more often than we think. We just have to start paying attention. How well do you know what your body is telling you? Try to connect, because it will help you to feel the unconditional love that is given to you and that you have to give. Your body will feel safe, relaxed, understood, and as big as the galaxy from the inside out.

Impact of Unconditional Love

With unconditional love, we would live like the stars in the galaxy. We would be at peace because we wouldn't have to fit into a group for survival and wouldn't have to prove to others that we are worthy.

There would be no pressure, and we would stop romanticizing love. With all that out of the way we could focus on the other feelings that love encompasses: compassion, empathy, understanding, support, self-confidence, generosity, faith in the future, self-respect, joy, letting go, trust, conflict without judgment, and passion.

We can start to change in that direction by having fewer expectations. We can begin with creating less stress and anxiety about what something should look like. Trust your inner voice.

It is the soft-spoken one, the one without judgment, the one that encourages you and tells you that change is positive and letting go of something is of great service.

This voice will never steer you wrong or make you do something that will hurt somebody else on purpose.

This voice is also the voice of your ability to express unconditional love. To love unconditionally doesn't mean that no matter what others say nor do, we have to agree and let it happen.

No, that is exactly what conditional love does. By loving unconditionally, you know you are a star in the sky, and so is everybody else. There is no one better or worse than you, and you are not better or worse than anyone else. You draw upon your strength and build up your weaknesses, while encouraging others to do the same.

You have healthy boundaries about what you will and will not tolerate. You respect other people's boundaries in return. You are willing to support somebody, but you refuse to carry their load for them. You feed the greatness in others, and you starve the victim and the martyr by not buying into their expectations. This way you help others empower themselves and give them the confidence to believe that they are worthy and that they can do whatever they need to do.

Sometimes we do the same thing over and over and expect a different outcome. According to Albert Einstein, that is the definition of insanity. When we give advice or tough love, we need to have no attachment to the outcome. The closer a person is to you, the more challenging it is to have no attachment or expectations.

At times, I find it difficult to stand by and say nothing when I see my family or clients making choices

that do not benefit them. I have to keep reminding myself that it is their life journey, not mine.
Examples of Unconditional Love

History has proven with the lives of different prominent figures, that unconditional love is not always the warm, fuzzy feeling, good kind of love. Jesus threw everybody out of the church. He viewed the church of the time as disrespectful to God. He also said to the sick, "heal thyselves."

Dr. Martin Luther King Jr. and Nelson Mandela were thrown in jail, physically abused, and they never threw a punch in self-defense. Mother Theresa helped the sick and the disabled, but she never viewed them as victims. Abraham Lincoln went to war to heal his beloved country and correct an injustice. Some actions are so impressive they set examples for us all.

Someone who says no to an addicted individual and refuses to support the addiction while still loving the person is practicing unconditional love.

A loved one is in an accident and is paralyzed, but by not treating them as victim and empowering them with support and unconditional love, this person becomes an Olympic athlete.

Someone helps a person with a mental or physical disability become the best he or she can be, that is unconditional love.

People who support teenage parents and help them become great parents without judging them and helping them find the resources they need, is practicing unconditional love.

A teacher who refuses to let students fall between the cracks of the system in practicing unconditional love in their profession.

Volunteers give their time and energy to help others succeed and thrive, be it as sports coaches to those delivering Meals on Wheels is demonstrating unconditional love for their community.

Unconditional love is about letting others make the mistakes they need to make in order to find their way, without you interfering or taking control. It is not taking responsibility away from someone when it is not your responsibility to assume. Unconditional love is about letting others use their talents, resources and inner wisdom to clean up their own messes, no matter how painful it may be watch. It is trusting others to do what only they know needs to be done, and letting them try and fail until they figure out how to succeed on their own, thus more fully equipping themselves with the tools they need to survive. Standing on the sidelines and supporting someone with their challenges is unconditional love.

This type of love is easy to understand when we put the **I Am status** into the five-point system. See the graph. Can you imagine what this does to a person and to the people around them when they relate from this frame of mind?

```
                    Trust/
                  Compassion

    Result /                      Conflict/
    Graceful      I AM            Honesty
                  STATUS

         Commitment/    Accountability/
          Spiritual       Visionary
```

For the graph, I used a part of my own **I Am status**, but you can fill it in for yourself. The moment we infuse the two together, we eliminate insecurity and make it is easier to see the greatness in everybody else. Our pets communicate this concept without words.

My dogs love me for who I am, not for how I look, where I live, what I do for a living, or what I said yesterday or what I promised to do tomorrow. They respond to how I treat them in the moment, and they are always happy when I'm home. I love my dogs, and I trained them to know I am their security, support and love.

I am their alpha (leader). As a pack animal, a dog's **I Am status** need an alpha figure to feel secure. If a dog doesn't have an alpha, it becomes alpha of itself and other pack members or family members. These dogs are considered unpredictable and dangerous because they don't have guidance or feel secure. We blame the dog for its unacceptable social behaviors. But what the dog is doing is compensating for the absence of security and love. If an owner does not understand how dogs relate and behave and does not train themselves to be the alpha and provide the love, security and support their dog needs, they can expect problem behaviors.

The same goes for our children when they are small. They need to feel the security that you will protect them, guide them, teach them and love them whatever happens or whatever they do. They trust us to teach them the skills they need in life. When we show unchanging affection without any conditions and guide with a firm hand, we have the best chance to successfully equip them with all the tools they need to know themselves, know their limits and be able to unconditionally love both themselves and others. Remember, everything needs love to succeed, grow, and flourish. It doesn't matter if it is a plant, an animal or a human.

Without love we wilt away, bit by bit, piece by piece. People who act obscenely, rudely and harm others, the people we find the most difficult to love are the ones who may need love the most. Maybe those people were never shown unconditional love or accepted for who they were? We all have people in our lives who we aren't sure deserve our love. We all have people we are not sure why or if we can ever love them. Keep in mind that maybe they think the same about you. I hear people say they want peace on earth, which is great, but we have to start with ourselves.

Love Your Self

Love yourself the way you are, expand and live from your **I Am status** then extend that love to the people around you. Forgive yourself and others for the mistakes that are made.

Whatever somebody tells you something, doesn't let it define you, be it positive or negative because often it is more about them than you. Watch your words, say only what you mean. Show respect for others' opinion and thoughts. And most important do the best you can in any given day with what you have available. If we all start with that premise, the world **will** become a better place.

Summary

- ✓ Love is the glue that holds everything together.
- ✓ Love is of great importance to our journey towards change.

- ✓ We need the feeling of love to safely encounter our fears of change.
- ✓ Love is always with us, but it is sometimes difficult to see because of our fears.
- ✓ We have power over which one we choose: love or fear.
- ✓ Love opens us up. Fear closes us down.
- ✓ We put the love we experience in life under the romantic-love umbrella, when it is so much more.
- ✓ We have been taught that we have to earn love and therefore love comes from the outside in and not from the inside out.
- ✓ We teach conditional love as being the true unconditional love.
- ✓ We learn about love from family, society, and media culture.
- ✓ When you are in the unconditional love mindset, you let go of expectations.
- ✓ To find happiness, joy, and peace, we have to switch from the conditional to the unconditional mindset.
- ✓ You feel unconditional love everywhere—in your heart, body, and mind.
- ✓ Everybody and everything needs unconditional love to grow into the magnificent beings they are.

CHAPTER 10

Steps You Can Take

In the first chapters I discussed why we think and act the way we do. Again - there is nothing wrong with you that you desperately need to fix. You are wonderful just the way you are.

This chapter provides you with a structure to go from a good life with struggles to a great life facing challenges. Your choice.

The concept is simple but will not always be easy. The people I know that have adopted this structure into their lives find their view on life is broadening since they started looking closely at their lives. They shed many unproductive beliefs.

You will discover more areas of your life that need attention. That is okay. That is what life is all about—you never stop learning about yourself and others.

Life is change. For creatures of habit, like humans, change is unnerving.

Let's look at how we can ride the waves of the unavoidable change, without fear.

Step 1: Be willing to see and live with yourself - no judgment, no fear, no struggle.

Sound too obvious and too simple? This is the most overlooked step in the process.

Recognizing change takes courage and open-mindedness. It is not for the faint of heart. Change makes many of us put our heads in the sand and pretend that nothing is happening. We look the other way.

You may not recognize your own fear reactions or fear-centered thoughts, but they will show up in your body language and the words you use. You will feel resentment and reluctance to deal with an issue. A common coping mechanism is pretending everything is the same or just fine. You are avoiding a change in your life.

Ask yourself - How can you acknowledge something when you refuse to look at it? You can't.

But when you are willing to acknowledge change and see it in your life, you create a starting point for yourself and the issues you are willing to face.

We often believe that we have no choice in what happens to us. That is not true. We may not have a choice in the changes that occur, but we always have a choice in how we deal with them.

For example, people get sick. Their body changes from well to ill. It is their choice how they react. They can choose to be mad, resentful, a victim, or even a martyr. But if they have the willingness to really look at their illness and acknowledge the limitations that it creates, they can also find opportunities to make their life easier while being ill and start to heal. They might say to themselves, "I am more than my body. I can still be productive by doing bookkeeping, answering the phone, and so on." If they focus on what they can do, not on what they can't, that attitude ripples through to the people around them.

By dealing with a difficult situation, like a long-term illness through acceptance of the situation and looking at the good and bad of the situation in the most positive way, the change and limitations you face can become opportunities, not tragedies. We all face limitations, no matter how well, or how smart or how rich we are. The key is to see them, live with them and make them a good thing.

Being willing in every situation to see the good, gives you more freedom to make lemonade when life hands you lemons.

But most of the time we are too afraid to look our challenges right in the eye and see not just the bad, but also find the good.

How do you become more willing, more able to face a challenge? When a life "obstacle" presents itself, when life doesn't go the way you wanted it to go, don't panic.

Stop and take a couple of deep breaths. After the breathing, do your best to observe the situation. Say to yourself, "I may not know how to deal with this, however, I am willing to see it."

The trick is to pause.

Pausing gives you the chance to plan your response to something, instead of reacting. If you find this unclear, look at the people around you, and observe how they handle difficult situations.

Find someone, like my Will and Sue, as examples to use in a difficult situation or change. If you have nobody to use as your example, then use stories from the media about those who battled their fear and moved on. Take a good look at nature. Over the last billion years nature has shown us how to adapt and be flexible when change occurs. See the tenacity of grass growing in a crack in the sidewalk, trees sprouting on the side of cliffs. We are surrounded by nature that has adapted to us. Take its example.

Ask yourself, "What is the worst that can happen right now?" After asking yourself that question, then stop, breathe, and think. The situation doesn't change, but the question creates an open spot with breathing room. You will feel more in control than you did and able to make better decisions. I've used this technique throughout most of my whole life, and it works for me. I've talked with friends and counseled clients who find it helps them respond with thoughtfulness, instead of reacting from fear.

Are you willing to try this?

Step 2: Create awareness.

Step 1 helps us be more relaxed in every situation. It gives us a clearer look at what we are facing. With a clear understanding of what we face, we have a choice about who controls our response, when saboteurs show up. Our saboteur will show up more, once you start to wonder what is your truth. Awareness happens when you question the things you have always taken for granted. You respond as your parents taught you, as society expects you to react.

The simplest way we create awareness is by paying attention to what and how we think. As stated in Chapter 3, everything starts with how we think. To increase our awareness of the change or fear we face, we have to look at what we think.

Observing Your Thoughts Exercise

There are many different ways of doing this. A simple way to start recognizing our habits of thinking is by meditation and while doing a task that doesn't take concentration, like cleaning the house or doing yard work.

The observation time can vary from a minute to ten minutes. The length of time depends on what you are doing and what interrupts you. When possible do this a couple of times a day. But do not beat yourself up if you have a difficult time starting this exercise; just keep reminding yourself that it will come, with practice. Don't give up; just be aware of what you are thinking as you sit still or while you are loading the washer or driving the car alone.

It will become easier over time. If it feels right for you, you can journal your findings as long as you don't get stressed out by this. You can get stressed if you think that in order for this exercise to work you have to do something a certain way. Tell your saboteur, "Thank you for sharing; however, this way works better for me," referring to whatever way works for you. The beauty of this exercise is that you don't have to do anything. Just observe. Becoming aware doesn't take over your daily life. If your life goal is understand yourself and others, start with yourself.

This book's goal is to help people take more control of their feelings and become clear about what is going on in and around them.

As you become more familiar with the kinds of thoughts that flit through your mind, you can start gently questioning your beliefs about your thoughts.

The following are some questions to consider while observing your thoughts:

- ✓ How often do I have a judgmental thought?
- ✓ What do I think about world politics?
- ✓ How often do I have a loving thought about myself or others?
- ✓ How do I view my work and coworkers?
- ✓ Do I love where I live?
- ✓ What are my thoughts about my body?
- ✓ Do I communicate my needs and wants with clarity?

These are just some examples. Please ask yourself the questions that are relative to your life and your goals. You might write them down on a recipe card to look at while meditating or have at the kitchen sink or car so you don't forget them.

The most important part is that you do the observing of your thoughts, without judgment. How you do it so it works for you, is up to you. It is just a support system. There is no timeline.

The more you practice, the quicker you will get it. Be patient with yourself, and have fun observing how you really think. You can't do this wrong, though your saboteur will tell you differently.

Power of Words

Once you have a clear idea about how and what you think, you can start the same observation technique on how you speak. Our thoughts are mostly private, but our words are public.

Words reveal our private thoughts as does how we say things. The words we speak have a huge impact on the people around us, more than we think they do.

Most of the time we don't see the direct impact our words have on others, but when we hear something often enough, we start to believe it.

For example, where did your beliefs about work come from? Where did you learn most of it? Was it from your parents?

You couldn't read their thoughts about work, but what did you hear them say and how did they talk about it? Were they happy, sad, angry or uncaring when they spoke about work? How did they handle it? What did you observe was important to them, when they talked about work to other people?

For many people, how their parents behaved about work and what they said about it formed the base of their beliefs.

This example can be applied to many things: relationships, how we treat people, how we love people or show our love, money etc. The important principal to remember is that what we hear others say over and over again, we start to believe and take on as the truth.

Mean words can leave lifetime scars, often ones that nobody can see. Repeated words and phrases do the same, they leave deep impressions that influence how we behave and react, not only on ourselves but with other people.

It is very important that we pay attention to what we say and how we say it. Start small and observe just one or two short conversations a day. The topics of those conversations don't need to be of great importance or significance. Keep the conversations you observe simple at first. Maybe observe yourself talking about the weather with a neighbor or someone you barely know or a discussion about your car needing an oil change with your spouse or a friend, etc.

Observing Our Words Exercise

When you feel you have a handle on how you speak in those conversations, Start to observe yourself in more elaborate conversations, like whose turn is it to pick up the kids, discussions about bills or the future.

As you get comfortable observing, not judging, how you talk with people, ask yourself,

"What do you notice?"

"Are you surprised at what you say and how you say it?"

Be honest with yourself. Always remember, this is not a test. You can't fail this. Nobody is judging you. The only reason for you to dive into this matter is to find out if the saboteur (insecurities) is in charge of your speech or your true self - your **I Am status**.

Now that you are comfortable with how you speak, start asking yourself questions to deepen your awareness.

- ✓ How do I voice my opinion about something I'm passionate about?
- ✓ How often do I speak lovingly about myself and others?
- ✓ How do I talk about my work and coworkers?
- ✓ Which tone of voice do I use when I talk about my home and family?
- ✓ What words do I use to describe my body?
- ✓ Do I communicate my needs and wants with clarity?
- ✓ How often do I speak with judgment?
- ✓ How often do I listen on Level 2 or Level 3?

Answer the above questions, not with the judgment of your saboteur but the observations of yourself. If you start to judge how you talk to others, tell your saboteur, "Thanks for sharing, but I am doing just fine doing this without your opinion."

With practice you will hear the difference between who is actually talking. When that happens, it will be a magical moment. In that moment you know that you can choose what you say and how you say it.

This level of awareness gives you the freedom of a new level of living. The phrase, "freedom of speech," will take on a whole new meaning for you. Nobody, not even your saboteur, will be telling you what to say and how to say it. It will be your glorious self. With your **I Am status** talking, you will show more compassion and consideration toward others and will be less judgmental and more open-minded.

If you doubt you can get it right, don't worry. There is a different method you can do to get to the same result.

When speaking, stop before you say something, and do your best not to say anything with a negative tone or message. The best way to do this is to fake it till you make it.

It may be difficult, but you can make a strong point without being negative and betraying yourself or agreeing to something you don't believe.

You don't have to agree with what your family or friends do or say. You can talk with them about the differences in your beliefs without being negative. The trick is to say what you want to say without making them wrong. The moment you tell or show somebody they are wrong, they feel defensive and are deaf to what you have to say. You appear to have formed your opinion and judgment about a situation. To learn about how to resolve situations such as this, read Chapter 11.

For now, you are learning how to face change and/or fear in your life, by first, watching what you say and how you say it, while always remembering you have a choice in how you respond.

By asking yourself, "What is the return I want out of this conversation?" on a regular basis, you discover that the more you pay attention to your thoughts and words, the more control you have over how you think and view the world. You also begin to communicate a more positive view to those around you.

Aligning Actions with Thoughts & Words
What about our actions?

Our actions are an embodiment of our thoughts and words. For the sake of observing how our actions influence our ability to respond, we can divide our actions into two categories:

> **Physical action** - what we actually do about how and what we consciously think and say.

> **Body language** - how we express our subconscious thoughts and words, through unintentional body movements.

Physical Actions

Let's first discuss the physical actions that we use to express how and what we think and feel. This is a very straightforward and easy to measurement - for example, how much progress we are making on a project. You get it done on time, or you don't. People are happy with what you've done, or they are not. You walk and train your dog, or you don't. You go to the gym three times a week or you do not.

By your actions or results, you communicate to others what you are capable of doing, the importance you place on an activity or how you feel about them or their actions. From these actions, you and others make judgments or guesses about what a person is likely to do or say in the future when you interact again.

Your actions are what others will be looking at when you interact with them. It is how they measure your progress and decide if you are doing what you said you would do. Based on physical action people decide if they can they trust your word on follow-up actions. Physical action demonstrates your ability to follow-through on your promises and commitments. Making goals and creating small steps toward those goals is action.

Physical action combined with our conscious thoughts and speech communicates our unconscious mindset. Our active communication is demonstrated in three dimensions - What we think and say will be visible in what we do.

For example, if you say you don't want others to judge you, but you gossip about others, you are saying what is proper in your family or society, but not practicing it. What does that communicate to others about your true nature?

If you say you want to quit smoking but light a smoke four times a day, what kind of message do you give others? You are telling people with your actions, not to trust your promises or feelings. Your actions indicate that you don't want to quit smoking.

You may tell people that you want to run a marathon but never do the training, registration or show up at the finish line. What are you communicating? You may be showing people you don't believe you can do it or that you don't really want to run the marathon.

When your thoughts, speech and physical actions are in sync, chances increase significantly that you can and are facing your inner fears, being aware of what you think, say and do and that you will do what you say you will.

If you say or think one thing and do something different, what message do you communicate to others? That is the question you have to ask yourself over and over again.

Observing Our Actions Exercise

The best way you can identify differences between what you say and what you do is by observing your actions. Start small. Just observe your actions for ten minutes a day.

After observing yourself, ask yourself these questions:

- ✓ Do I take small steps toward my goal?
- ✓ What am I thinking, and is that helping or hindering my actions?
- ✓ How do I speak, and is that in line with my actions?
- ✓ What is the biggest benefit for me when my thoughts and speech match my actions?

If you want to journal on this, great, but again you don't have to. If you do journal, you always have a reference point you can use when you are further along on your new path.

When you are comfortable, add another ten minutes of observing your thoughts, speech and actions, and increase it as needed.

What do you notice?

Try to be unbiased and have compassion for yourself. We are working on becoming more aware. It takes time and will not happen overnight. Enjoy and learn from this journey. If you fall off the wagon, just laugh and get back on. Don't feel bad when you fall. Observe and keep practicing to align your actions with your thoughts and words.

Actions always speak louder than words.

Body Language

At least 60 percent of our communication is done by body language. We don't pay enough attention to this form of communicating, even though it is a huge part of how we interact and are perceived by others. Subconsciously, we constantly read each other's body language. We ask in a split second - does this person mean harm or not? What kind of mood is he or she in? Does this person enjoying his or her job? All these questions and more go through our minds every time we walk into a situation. We use the body for silent communication, and that is a form of action.

When you are joyful, your posture will be open and relaxed. You may talk with your hands and smile. Every person you meet will smile back, even when he or she is not in a joyful mood.

Try this:

As you go through your day, smile at somebody, and see what they do.

When you look angry, the person you meet will avoid you or look back angrily.

How often do you pay attention to what vibes you send out with your body? Were you even aware that you do that?

We all comment once in a while about what we observe in somebody else. You may say something like "Do you know what was wrong with Bob? He looked angry (worried, sad, embarrassed, closed off, so on)?" Bob didn't say anything, but you could see that he was not happy. You are reading Bob's body language.

If you can read people's body language without them saying anything, they can read yours. We are so busy these days that we often forget to reset our body posture. When you work in a store and you've just dealt with a frustrating customer, sometimes you forget to re-adjust your body language. While your words may be friendly, your body communicates a different message. This can cost you more than a confused client. It can cost you a sale and a repeat customer.

Dealing with children or parents can be challenging. Several people may be in the same room at the same time when someone makes you angry. How do you reset yourself, when others are present?

Body Language Exercises

Observe your body language for five minutes. Just observe no judgment. Examine how you hold yourself - are you relaxed or stiff? Look in the mirror - what is your facial expression and what mood does it communicate? Start when you are alone and build on your observations.

If possible, have conversations where you can observe yourself, without attention. Is your body saying the same thing as your mouth and physical actions? If that is awkward for you, start by observing others, and when you get a handle on that, go back and start observe yourself. If that is still difficult for you to do, ask a trusted partner or friend, what they see in your body posture.

Body language is a huge part of communication, so it important to spend the time on understanding how you communicate with your facial expressions, posture and movements. You want to eventually know that your thoughts, words, physical actions and body language are aligned when you are talking with others.

Body language is what people see first. When you do an action that you resent doing, those feelings of resentment will show in your facial expressions and body positions. Mothers and fathers often rely on their children's body language to understand what was unspoken. It is how most parents raise their children; it is something they do subconsciously. My children could never understand how I knew when they had done something wrong or if they were lying. Their words and actions did not line up with what their body was saying. In poker, it is called a tell. It is a movement and/or expression you make in certain situations.

Interpreting Body Language

To understand your body language, pay attention to your body sensations and inner voice. Observation helps you trust your inner wisdom.

Our bodies give us clues all the time, and nine times out of ten we dismiss them as unimportant. Later we say to a friend after something happened to us, "Why we didn't see it coming." Sometimes we will even acknowledge we had a weird feeling about it. That was your body telling you, "Stop. Don't go further. This is not good."

The best way to strengthen this awareness is to practice by starting small. Ask yourself questions like:

- ✓ Which are the best socks to wear today?
- ✓ What is my body craving right now?
- ✓ Is this the right program for me to watch?
- ✓ What is the best book for me to read?

Ask a question, stop, and observe the answer you are getting from your body. Follow that suggestion and see what happens next.

The answers to these questions are not important. It is not a matter of life and death if you wear black socks instead of green ones, no matter what your saboteur says.

Notice what your inner voice has to say and how your body feels in the moment. Over time, you may surprise yourself with the findings.

By listening to your inner voice and following its advice, that voice will become clearer, louder, and more trustworthy over time.

Don't give up if you get nothing. Chances are that you're just trying too hard. Ask questions that aren't emotionally important to you and follow your own advice. When you trust your inner voice, start asking more complex questions like:

- ✓ Is this the right relationship for me?
- ✓ What do I really want to do?
- ✓ Which actions do I need to take to get to my Vancouver?
- ✓ What will make me happy and peaceful?
- ✓ What do I want from my partner?
- ✓ What is the best way to work with this difficult co-worker?

Now when you ask the more advanced questions, slowly focus on your body sensations.

- ✓ Are your muscles contracted or relaxed?
- ✓ Are you hot or cold?
- ✓ Do you have a tingling or warm feeling?

Notice all of the sensations, and concentrate on feeling as much as you can.

In this space ask advice from your inner wisdom, and listen to what it has to say. Try not to interrupt or dismiss what you are told. In the beginning, I advise writing down what your inner wisdom has to share so you have a reference point that exists outside of you.

Sometimes it is helpful to have notes to refer back to when gauging your progress.

At time it is easier to detach and avoid judgment or the urge to ignore the message when it is outside of you instead in your head. Writing these thoughts and feelings down allows you to go back and read what you wrote. At times, you will be amazed at the wisdom you possess.

If it is too scary for you or you are not ready to follow your own recommendations, you can always dismiss your instincts and choose another action. Keep track of the outcome to help you observe yourself and the results.

Your inner voice may give you answers you don't want to hear or that you think is too much to ask for. Whatever it is, you can do it. You never get more than you can handle, although there are times that what happens seems to be more than we believe we can ever deal with.

Going within for answers may not always provide easy or popular answers. You need to grow your faith in your inner wisdom and believe that you are capable of understanding and doing exactly what you need on your journey to find peace and happiness.

This is not selfish. This is a necessity for creating personal peace, and therefore, world peace. They are so intertwined that you can't see the one without the other. The reason there is no peace on earth is because we ourselves are not at peace. To change the world we have to start with ourselves. The best way of doing that is to first know and trust ourselves.

Observation of Habits

Habits are a type of body language. It is a routine we perform on a regular basis, almost without thought. Observing your habits can reveal more of yourself to you. Pay attention to your habits by starting small and observing your morning or night routines. Often we don't even realize that we have a routine till we shine a light on it.

Sometimes the way we interact with others involves a habit or routine. Often we talk to our children differently than the way we talk to our parents, coworkers or somebody on the street.

Masks We Wear and Why

The differences originate in our perception that we have to fulfill different expectations in each interaction to fit in or achieve a desired result. We divide ourselves into different personalities and believe we have to behave according to the different roles we play. These roles become masks we assume with each other.

How do we keep on the mother mask in front of a client or co-worker? Can we be the same with our children as we are with our friends?

To keep true to our **I Am status,** we don't have to share the same information in every group, but we do need to act from the same inner place all the time. We should aim to spend every moment of our lives as we truly are - communicating from our **I am status.**

When we divide ourselves into different personas, our life becomes a circle with many different masks. Which masks do you wear? Are they the same as in the graph below?

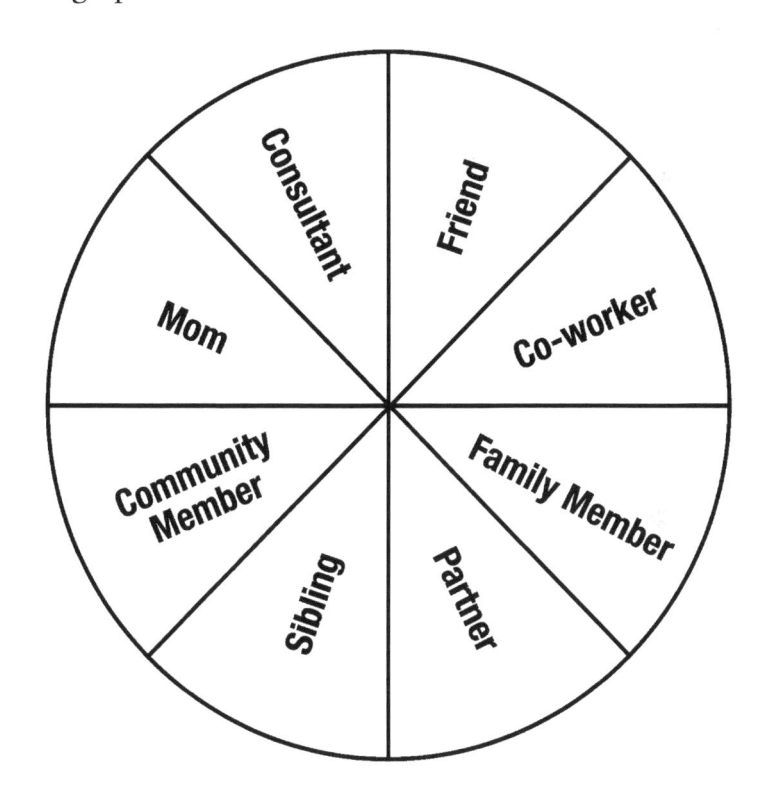

(Diagram: a circle divided into eight segments labeled Consultant, Friend, Co-worker, Family Member, Partner, Sibling, Community Member, Mom.)

Did you come up with the same masks I did? On a typical day how often do you put a different mask on?

I've never counted the masks I assume or those my clients wear, but it is more then we realize. Masks hide our **I Am status** behind different behaviors we believe are necessary to succeed in communicating with each different peer group.

Each mask is a piece of the puzzle that is you. Each mask holds glimpses of your beautiful inner being, regardless of which role you are playing. It's like you are a puzzle hanging on the wall with a different puzzle on each side that are similar but not connected. With just unconnected puzzle pieces to work with, it is difficult to complete the puzzle and see our most precious possession, our **I Am status** whole, with no gaps, no pretensions.

What would happen if we stopped hiding behind these incomplete masks?

What would happen we were the same all the time, no matter whom we interacted with?

Your **I am status** would become complete, like the puzzle, and you would discover the big picture and all the great qualities that you possess but did not connect. It would be easier to be you're wonderful glorious self. And instead of your own worst enemy, you could become your own best friend.

Start Finding Who You Are

It is possible, but it takes small steps. Don't start observing your thoughts, words, action and habits all at once. You will put your saboteur in overdrive and probably judge yourself harshly. Such action would stall your journey.

Be gentle on yourself. Keep it simple and observe yourself one facet at a time. Master the art of meditation and hearing your thoughts. Not judging, just hearing them. Then move on to watching your words. Observe what you say, then how you say it with your physical actions. Once you are aware of physical actions, tune into your body language. Then examine your habits.

There is no hurry. Be consistent and forgive yourself when you lapse. Do your best to observe one of the five ways of communicating at least once a day. Keep moving forward at your pace and have fun. Don't take everything too seriously.

Always remember **there is nothing wrong with you that you have to fix.** You are only observing what you are communicating. From the previous chapters, you understand that under the layers of family, society, media and experience, exists who you truly are and have always been - your **I Am status**.

As you observe, you will understand yourself better. Your next step is to determine what are your findings, and what are you going to do with them?

Being aware creates choices. You can decide how to respond to any situation.

You may find your saboteur is so powerful that you run away scared and don't want to look further. That is okay. It is always your choice.

But if you want to feel even lighter than you do now, you can do deeper exercises.

Here are some evaluative questions you can ask yourself.

- ✓ What did you discover?
- ✓ What was the biggest surprise?
- ✓ How was the process for you?
- ✓ How often did you want to quit?
- ✓ What came up for you?
- ✓ What did your saboteur tell you during the process?
- ✓ Are your thoughts, words, actions, and habits a roadmap to your Vancouver or to Halifax?
- ✓ What are your biggest fears?

You are on a hero's journey. Start gently and truthfully look at yourself. The hero - you - is a real, authentic person who is afraid but still willing to look at themselves and figure out how they have to do to change themselves and change the world.

It is normal to feel overwhelmed by your observation or hear your saboteur thinking things for you like "I am just one person, I can't change the world."

I know you can change and change the world, because I've seen it happen in my life and the lives of others. When you become more aware and live as a hero (honoring your **I Am status**), you will change, and people will be drawn to you. Even those unsettled by the change they see and hear, especially people close to you. The ripple effect changes the world. When you live from your **I Am status** and see it in others, you give others permission to live from their authentic self.

This is the secret to a peaceful world. By honoring yourself and others for the remarkable beings they are without judgment, your fear, anger and judgment fades. Solutions, with the contribution of many voices and viewpoints arise, because all are being heard.

Step 3: Practice gratitude.

What are you grateful for during the day? It is easy to be thankful for the great things in life. Are you grateful for the difficult obstacles you encounter in life? Probably not. The biggest rewards lie in the struggle to overcome difficulties.

How great do you feel when you accomplish something challenging?

It can be personal, physical, work-related, hobby, or family-related. When you first see the problems, you want to turn around and walk away. When you can't do that, you have only one choice, and that's to deal with it. We all get stronger from what we conquer. I have seen that over and over again in my family, my life coaching and my friends. In the deepest valleys of life, we find our inner strength and wisdom. That is something for which to be grateful.

Look at challenging episodes in your life. Focus on what you learned from that experience. Don't analyze the event; just notice what you learned from it. Start slowly with an uncomfortable episode, and work yourself up to the most difficult episodes of your life. Go from the light gray times in your life to the events you see as black in your mind.

Can you find something to be grateful for in each instance?

Remember to always be compassionate and non-judgmental with yourself, and have the faith that you can find the silver lining in your dark clouds. A load, you may not have known you were carrying, will be lifted off you, and you will feel lighter. That is the power of gratitude.

Practice gratitude every day. Start with the small, easy thank-you's, and work toward being thankful for the more difficult situations. Keep a notepad next to your bed and write three things a day that you are grateful for and write out your feelings about the big events in your life. You may be amazed what you will discover about yourself and life itself.

These simple exercises help you focus on you and your **I Am status**, in the present, revealing the patterns you've developed in life. When you expose your old beliefs, you can choose which ones are beneficial and which ones are not.

Let go of the beliefs holding you back and free yourself. Gratitude enables you to be proud of yourself for having the courage to observe and discover your life. You may not always be in control of life events, but with these tools you always know how to respond to the curves and rewards that life constantly provides you.

Step 4 - Changes

Keep in mind that there is nothing wrong with you.
Evaluate your findings. With information on how you operate, is there something in your life you want to modify?

If so, do the same exercises, but instead of observing, start doing. Start thinking about different possibilities. Map them out in your mind. Start changing what you say and do and new habits will follow.

Optional: Pen, notepad or journal, and maybe tissues
Step 1: Be willing to look at your life.
Step 2: Create awareness.
Step 3: Practice Gratitude
Step 4: Create the changes you desire

Summary

- ✓ Observe your thoughts for one to five minutes. Don't question or judge them. Notice your thought pattern, and ask if it serves you well. Start building on the observation in different settings and lengthening the observation time. Practice makes perfect.
- ✓ Writing your findings down is optional. Some people find it helpful. This counts for the rest of the exercises as well.
- ✓ Observe your words. Start with an easy conversation, and build toward a more difficult conversation.
- ✓ Be gentle. Don't judge. Keep breathing. All is well. Slowly lengthen
- ✓ the observation time when you feel more comfortable with the procedure.
- ✓ Observe your physical actions. What is it that you actually do? Start
- ✓ small and build on that.
- ✓ Observe your body language. Is it in harmony with what you think, say and do in that moment?
- ✓ Pay attention to your body sensations and inner voice. Start feeling what goes on inside of you. Don't push it away or judge it. Just observe and take mental notes.

- ✓ Observe your habits.
- ✓ Evaluate your findings. With information on how you operate, is there something in your life you want to modify? If so, do the same exercise, but instead of observing, start doing. Start thinking about
- ✓ different possibilities. Map them out in your mind. Start paying attention to what you say and do, and new habits will follow.
- ✓ Practice gratitude for everything—the small things, the wonderful events, and the learning we gain from difficult, dark events. Some examples are:
- ✓ Having a coffee in the sun
- ✓ Finding the right-fitting clothes for an occasion
- ✓ Birth of a child
- ✓ Surviving an accident
- ✓ Losing a job
- ✓ Unfair situations.
- ✓ If there is something you want to change, do the same exercises, but instead of observing, start doing. Start thinking about different possibilities. Map them out in your mind. Start changing what you say and do and new habits will follow.

CHAPTER 11
Rewards and Reactions

What is the reward for becoming aware, going inside, and facing all those fears? What good does it do?

My clients and I have noticed that while doing the exercises and looking at ourselves, the people around us start to frustrate us with their short-sightedness.

It feels like they fight every step we take, and they don't understand my clients or me. They criticize by telling us to be normal.

Those who have followed the exercises to uncover their **I Am status** find their friends and loved ones don't want to listen to them. They feel unable to talk about their journey.

The reactions of others in our life often causes us to ask the question - If exploring who I really am and facing the change and fears in my life causes fights with my partner and friends - Why is this good for me?

The exercises are simple but not easy to do. The process causes a ripple effect. You have a calm lake and a stone. Each is non-threatening on its own. But when you throw the stone and it hits the water, the waves start. You have changed the dynamic between the lake and the stone, and it won't be the same.

Can you bring the lake back to exactly how it was before? You may see a calm surface eventually but when you look through a microscope, you will see that the molecules are not in the same position.

What about the stone? Even when we pick the same stone out of the lake, we never can put it back exactly where we found it.

You are the stone, and everybody around you is the lake. The moment you move, you will influence those around you. This happens whether you are aware of it or not. It is an ongoing occurrence. This is life itself.

The next question you may ask yourself is - If this is life, why would I want to become more aware and deal with more frustration? What is wrong with the way I live now?

Absolutely nothing.

It is all about choice. I have discussed different pieces of the puzzle. When you bring them all together, imagine a double-sided puzzle, each side with a different picture. One side could be flowers and the other a busy street. Both are beautiful and have charm on their own.

When you start making the puzzle, you have to decide which side you are going to piece together. You can't work on both sides at once, even though that's technically what you're doing. When you pick up a piece, you have to look to see which side it is before you can find its place. As you solve one side, you are solving the other.

Life is one of those puzzles. We can live a life unaware of the influences around us that determine how we react or we can live a life aware of those influences and how they determine how we respond. Both are present. It is up to you which end result you prefer.

Before we start solving the puzzle, let's lay out all the pieces:

- ✓ Five-Point System,
- ✓ I Am status,
- ✓ Family culture,
- ✓ Societal culture,
- ✓ Reactions - blame, shame, and guilt feelings,
- ✓ Comfort zone,
- ✓ Wants and needs,
- ✓ Validation,
- ✓ Personal Vancouver
- ✓ Resistance.

To complicate things, all the pieces are used for each side of the puzzle, but the picture is different based on the point of view. This is the most difficult puzzle you will ever solve. Most of us don't even know that we are working on this puzzle.

Unawareness Puzzle

What does the puzzle picture without awareness look like? To put together that image, we have to work with some clues each piece gives us.

Five-Point System

- ✓ You teach your children the same values that were taught to you.
- ✓ You only look at the world from your point of view.
- ✓ You don't know that there is insecurity in your system.
- ✓ You run away from your fears.
- ✓ Outside events just happen to you.

I-Am Status

- ✓ You can't find your toolbox.
- ✓ You don't know what your **I Am status** is.
- ✓ You are taught that looking after yourself is selfish.

Family Culture

- ✓ Everything that your family says or does is normal.
- ✓ You believe that what others say is always the truth. They are the experts.
- ✓ You do things because that's the way they have always been done.

Societal Culture

- ✓ You don't question what you do.
- ✓ You do the same things over and over again.
- ✓ You play by the rules. In return you are accepted.

Reactions

- ✓ You talk before you understand what the other person is telling you.
- ✓ You jump to conclusions.
- ✓ You don't ask questions.
- ✓ You assume that your point of view is the only right one.

Blame, Shame, and Guilt Feelings

- ✓ You don't see different options.
- ✓ You do things out of duty.

- ✓ You incorporate others' expectations in your vision.
- ✓ You don't trust your inner wisdom.
- ✓ You operate from somebody else's standards.

Comfort Zone

- ✓ You always play safe.
- ✓ You don't want to rock the boat.
- ✓ You are satisfied with what life has to give you.

Wants and Needs

- ✓ You are afraid to communicate what you really want.
- ✓ You are afraid of what others will think.
- ✓ You don't know what you want.

Validation

- ✓ You are not self-confident.
- ✓ You adopt others' points of view.
- ✓ You are not open to feedback.

Personal Vancouver

- ✓ You don't really have goals and dreams.

- ✓ You are afraid of offending others with your deepest desires.
- ✓ You are afraid of disappointing yourself.

Resistance

- ✓ You are afraid of change.
- ✓ You are afraid of conflict.
- ✓ You are afraid of failure.

When you look closely, you can see that some pieces flow over into another like with a real puzzle. I can't tell you the exact picture on your personal puzzle, because it all depends on the degree you engage with all the pieces above. What I see when observing, working with or in relationships with people who are unaware of themselves is the following:

- ✓ They feel the need to defend themselves.
- ✓ They are closed off to feedback.
- ✓ They are always right, and the other is wrong.
- ✓ Failure is not an option.
- ✓ Living small is the way to go.
- ✓ To be good they have to behave according to society's standards.
- ✓ They fly under the radar.
- ✓ They put too much value on others' opinions.
- ✓ They restrict themselves from truly living.

The colors of this puzzle will be dark shades of blue, green, gray, brown, and red with some lighter shades of yellow and orange. This image is heavy, stale, unmoving, and fearful. It contains much drama, with few light points.

Most people (even you) will choose this image because this is the one you see everywhere. It is familiar and comforting. It is a life so focused on the life events that happen to us that we forget to look inside. That is what this side of the puzzle represents.

Awareness Puzzle

What does the puzzle picture with awareness look like? To put together that image, we have to work with the clues each piece gives us to see the difference between the two puzzles.

Five-Point System

- ✓ You know what the five points mean in your life.
- ✓ You do your best to teach the five points to your children.
- ✓ You admit when you make a mistake.

I-Am Status

- ✓ You are self-confident.
- ✓ You know your toolbox and work with it.

- ✓ You have a healthy balance of looking after yourself and others.

Family Culture

- ✓ You let your children make their own mistakes.
- ✓ You trust that what you taught your children will help them live life.
- ✓ You respect your parents for what they taught you, but you follow your own path in life.

Societal Culture

- ✓ You respect others' opinion, but you still do what is good for you.
- ✓ You know the impact you have on the world around you.
- ✓ You make decisions that are good for you and the people around you.

Reactions

- ✓ Before you reply, you stop, think, and then respond.
- ✓ You ask when, what, where, and how questions.
- ✓ You don't assume. You ask questions.

Blame, Shame, and Guilt Feelings

- ✓ You look at where these feelings originated.
- ✓ You are thankful for the lessons they've taught you.
- ✓ You release those feelings with respect.
- ✓ You don't take everything personally.

Comfort Zone

- ✓ You explore the world with an open mind.
- ✓ You are willing to ask for help. All sources count.
- ✓ You are curious, instead of judgmental.

Wants and Needs

- ✓ Your goals and dreams are clear.
- ✓ Personal boundaries are in place.
- ✓ You have no attachment to what something should look like.

Validation

- ✓ You validate others the way you do yourself.
- ✓ You do your best to see situations from other people's viewpoints.
- ✓ You are confident in your point of view.

Personal Vancouver
- ✓ You know where you want to go.
- ✓ You are flexible and adapt to changes.
- ✓ You embrace your inner greatness.

Resistance

- ✓ You are open-minded to new ideas and options.
- ✓ You face fears head on.
- ✓ You are willing to think outside the box.

This is what I see when I observe people who are aware:

- ✓ They have their personal Vancouver in sight at all times.
- ✓ They are more forgiving.
- ✓ They are more open-minded.
- ✓ They live by their own greatness and encourage others to do the same.
- ✓ They are less judgmental.
- ✓ They know the difference between encouraging and doing things for others.

The colors on this puzzle are the lighter shades of green, blue, yellow, orange, pink, and red with some gray and brown. This picture is light, upbeat, like a summer bouquet of flowers, and understanding with a serious undertone.

The majority of humanity loves this image and wants it as their own. The biggest obstacle in achieving this is that you have to face your inner fears. This side of the puzzle represents thinking for ourselves, not following the crowd, being a leader, and encouraging others to find and live in their own greatness.

Both Sides Are Fine

There is nothing wrong with either side of the puzzle. As long as you understand that there is a choice to make, then it doesn't matter which side you choose. You will simply get different outcomes. The outcome you desire will determine what the best choices are for you. Ask yourself, is what I'm doing now the road to my personal Vancouver or to Halifax?

Dealing With the Ripples of Your Actions

Remember the ripples we make in life? Now you know that you have options for what kind of influence you spread. If you choose awareness, on average you won't get a lot of recognition for this or awards like the Nobel Peace Prize. It is not a glorious path that leads to fame and wealth. This choice does not come with a guarantee that you never will find hardship in life.

You will encounter others who don't understand you, find you weird, and even judge you. There is a chance you could lose some of the friends you have now because they can't handle the new you. You may not be comfort with the old them.

What is the plus side?

Awareness makes you less judgmental. You show more compassion. You thrust your inner wisdom, experience inner freedom and peace into whatever life brings you.

There is choice in everything that comes your way, not the events themselves but the way you respond to them. Your **I Am status** becomes your guide in life. Your choice makes you an example for others to follow, especially when your thoughts, words, actions, and habits are all on the same page and in line with your **I Am status.** When you operate from your **I Am status**, you don't practice the ability to hurt others. That doesn't mean that the others can't feel hurt. Hurt is created by how you perceive what somebody is telling you. A strong **I Am status** always speak from love even when it is tough love. Another plus is that you don't waste energy on negative self-talk or engage in gossip. This frees you up to dealing with the challenge at hand and allows you to move on.

What is the impact of all this on daily life?

If you've never heard of becoming aware or are not interested, then nothing will change your reactions to life. You will always be afraid of the life events that push you out of your comfort zone. This process makes us afraid, and the reactions we have will show that.

Living on this planet is makes us aware of ourselves and our relationship with others. So why not become actively aware so that when life events happen, you have the tools to respond instead of a panic reaction?

Reading this far makes it almost impossible for you to go back to your life as it was before you picked up this book. Somewhere in the future you will remember something you read here that will resonate with and apply to your life. You have already thrown the stone and rippled the lake.

Awareness of Others

The effect of your awareness will go on and on. We looked at the first stage - the impact of awareness on ourselves. Now it is time to expand that and look at the effects on the people around us.

Let's start with family life. Families are so interconnected that they all affect the others in the group. Keep in mind that awareness is nothing more than you knowing your glorious self, your hidden fears and insecurities. When you first start the process of looking at your inner fears and false beliefs, you may feel like a runaway train with no brakes. This is normal.

Now the domino effect comes into play. When you feel off, the rest of the family will be impacted. Your partner may be frustrated with work, or your children may not want to cooperate.

Your saboteur will always find events that will explain why the others at this point are a pain in your behind. It will search for evidence that the problem is always them. This way of thinking steers you away from your own inner fears and insecurities, and the saboteur's job is done. It has deflected responsibility from itself and placed it on others. The focus will be redirected to the other, who will become the target of your fears, and that's when you start blaming the people closest to you. In short, when others in the group irritate you, it is time to examine your own state of mind and what it is in you that is fearful and needs attention.

Ripple Effect in Families

The mirror neurons mentioned in Chapter 10 work this way. You see something, and you mirror that, whether it is a smile or a frown. If your mother is in a bad mood, so are you within twenty minutes. This response is most noticeable among the people you are the closest to like parents, children, and co-workers.

When you pay attention, you can detect mirror neurons at work in any situation. In family settings, when one person is off, it affects everybody. Events like illness or losing a job cut deep into a family. The children will look to the caregiver for guidance; It is up to the caregiver to mirror strength and courage, even when that is difficult. The best you can do is try to explain what is going on in simple terms and say that you are dealing with the situation.

If there is friction between partners, don't bring your kids into it. Do your best to stay parents of the children even when you aren't partners anymore. The only way you can do that is to always put the children's interests first. This may seem obvious, but sadly it is not often done. We are so wrapped up in ourselves in difficult times that we forget the children who depend on us. So many examples exist but what they all have in common is that in unawareness we try to control everybody around us in order to feel safe and in control.

If you are a parent, and the kids get into paint left out by another adult and paint themselves, the walls and the floor, who are you really mad at? After yelling at the kids and banishing them to their bedrooms, sit back and look at the situation, your thoughts, your words and your actions. You might come to the following conclusions.

- ✓ You were mad at the guys for not cleaning up the paint.
- ✓ You were mad you didn't watch the kids because you had other work to that you didn't really want to do
- ✓ You were mad at the adults for not paying attention to the kids.
- ✓ You were mad because you were tired from a hectic day and just wanted rest.

Many parents, uncomfortable or tired with the demands of parenting, feel the need to be in control of their children and their partner and those around them, instead of acknowledging the real reason they get upset.

You can't control the people around you, so their frustrations get expressed on the easiest, most obvious and available audience-the children. This example shows how we can reset ourselves when we experience a frustrating situation

First, we have to acknowledge that we are aware people control themselves and therefore use their inner wisdom and courage to respond to difficult situations the best they can. Here are some tips on how to do that:

- ✓ Be clear and honest about what you are feeling.
- ✓ Acknowledge and be clear about what you are upset about.
- ✓ Share what you are upset about, focusing on how what happened impacted you.
- ✓ Give yourself space to respond. Count to ten. Go to the washroom with a book.
- ✓ Distract yourself. Look at something else very closely for fifteen seconds.
- ✓ See the other person as a special individual.

The five-point system helps us use those tips. This system helps us gauge how we are doing keeping insecurity out of our lives. Think about it: the clearer and therefore more aware we are of trust, accountability, commitment, healthy conflict, and results, the better we can teach our children and others the system. If we want others to do as we ask, we have to model the behavior by doing it first.

How can I tell my 18 year-old son not to drink and drive if I get drunk and drive home?

How can I ask my mom not to gossip if I always talk negatively about others?

We can't do one thing and teach another. You may say, "But I try all the time, and it is not working." It is, or it is not. There is no in-between. If you tell me you're trying to do your best, that doesn't work. When you try, you don't make a decision about which way you want to go. You mirror that to the people around you, so they are held in limbo by your contradictory actions of saying one thing and doing another. The only thing you can promise yourself is that you are doing the best you can at any given moment with the tools you have.

Living With Awareness

Considering our influence on others, what does living with awareness look like in daily life?

Let's start with your **I Am status.** When you have access to your **I Am status**, you mirror that to the people around you. By standing in inner power and peace you encourage others to do the same. Keep in mind that subconsciously you mirror this outward.

A disconnect can happen when people in your life see the inner power and feel threatened by it. This happens more than we think. When we encounter a person with inner peace, we can't believe what we see. We often dismiss their peace or attitude as fake and will do anything to squash the power that is displayed. To make the confusion complete, we can come from an aware point of view one moment while the saboteur has a hold of us the next.

So what is inner power? What is the saboteur?

Only aware people can answer that question about themselves. As a coach I can hear it when I am coaching somebody. Listening to them talk I hear it in their voice. When the saboteur is talking, the voice goes flat and gets defensive, while the voice of inner wisdom has a light, passionate, compassionate tone. It is possible to mirror both the saboteur and the **I Am status** multiple times a day. We are complex creatures.

When it is hard for us to detect in ourselves which one is talking, how can we know which part of our partners is talking? On average we just don't know, it is more of a guess. That's why it is so important to do these four things, when seeking awareness.

- ✓ Do your best every day,
- ✓ Don't take everything personally,
- ✓ Watch what you say
- ✓ Don't assume.

When dealing with someone, simply look and see the **I Am status** in the person in front of you. Don't question or judge that statement in any situation. I haven't met anybody yet who doesn't have an **I Am status** buried somewhere deep inside them. These statements can help you find their **I Am status:**

- ✓ I know their **I Am status** is in there.
- ✓ This person has insecurities and fears just like me.
- ✓ This person knows what's best for him or herself.
- ✓ This person is mirroring something to me right now.
- ✓ This person has goals and dreams and is whole just the way he or she is.
- ✓ Everybody deserves to be treated with respect and dignity.
- ✓ I need to address the person, not his or her behavior.
- ✓ I don't have to fix this person, because there is nothing wrong with them.

Doing this will be the start of a new way to see and interact with others. You can dismiss the glory and the greatness in the other, only when you are controlled by your own inner insecurities, when your personal five-point system, family, societal, and media cultures and insecurities are intertwined.

Let's look at the five-point system right now. I've discussed how the system is the gauge for how aware we personally are. In daily life this is taking full responsibility for all the five points at any given time and any given moment. This makes it impossible to blame anyone for what is wrong in our lives. Remember, they only mirror to us what we need to become aware of.

- ✓ When we don't trust our own inner wisdom 100 percent, we can't trust others. Mirror: Others can't trust us 100 percent.
- ✓ We are not 100 percent accountable. Mirror: Others don't trust that we are 100 percent accountable.
- ✓ We don't know healthy conflict. Mirror: Others don't know healthy conflict either.
- ✓ We don't commit 100 percent. Mirror: Others won't commit 100 percent either.
- ✓ We don't know what kind of result we want out of life. Mirror: Others don't know what they want out of life.

This makes the people around us our best teachers on the lessons we need to learn. If we choose to work on our own five-point system, how will mirroring show us what we need to learn?

- ✓ We trust our inner wisdom and so trust others till proven differently. Mirror: We encourage others to trust as well.
- ✓ We are accountable. Mirror: We encourage others to be accountable as well.
- ✓ We are committed. Mirror: We encourage others to be committed as well.
- ✓ We know the power of healthy conflict. Mirror: We encourage others to do the same.
- ✓ We know our personal Vancouver. Mirror: We encourage others to share their Vancouver with us.

From this stand point we will handle situation with an open mind and we become curious on about where other people are coming from. It becomes difficult for you to cheat and lie, because you know the power of awareness and mirroring. When you hurt others, you will feel it as well.

Your **I Am status** is connected to all other's **I Am statuses**. When you hurt somebody, your **I Am status** will feel attacked. When you inflict a wound on somebody, you will have used a knife that stabs both you and the other person. You may not be aware of this, and sometimes the wound may take a long time to catch up with you, but eventually it will. The concept that when you hurt others, you hurt yourself is often a difficult one for people to see because the consequences may not be immediately visible.

For example:

Childhood trauma inflicted by parents: By the time we reach thirty-five to forty-five we start evaluating our lives. Unresolved trauma, as talked about through the book, will come to the front of our consciousness even if we can't name it. It often surfaces as resentment and blame. To give this an outlet we mirror this back at our parents, which can confuse the parents because they don't understand why they deserve this treatment from their children. Of course this is not clearly communicated between the two parties, and continues in a circle with both parties hurting and blaming each other.

Conflict between partners. By believing your partner to be wrong in their point of view and refusing to consider their point of view, we may believe we are winning the argument. In the long term, we create self-righteousness and distance. Relationship often fails that have developed distance between partners too great to be bridged.

Conflict between family members: Due to unclear communication and expectations fighting and separation can occur.

Judgment inflicted on behavior: By judging someone's behavior or actions you put them in the wrong, triggering their defensive action, which can escalate into fighting and isolation.

By our actions we choose our own destiny. We can't choose our life events, just our response to them. We are responsible for our own lives, thoughts, speech, action, and habits. Nobody else can do it for us, even if we think they can.

By giving another the responsibility over our lives, we hand over our power of choice. If parents don't let children make their own mistakes (no matter the age), they don't teach children responsibility for themselves. We can learn the most from our mistakes and failures. The best thing we can do for the next generation is teach them not to quit when they make a mistakes or fail. We should not judge what they do but show them, by our actions, how to learn from an action.

Too often we are so busy judging and condemning mistakes that we fear trying something new or different. Our lives circle, lost in the fear that keeps us from moving ahead.

Stopping this cycle starts with us. Taking full responsibility of life - its mistakes, failures, and successes and observing (not judging) ourselves and others enables us to learn from every situation presented to us. This is how we live on the awareness side of life's puzzle. This way of life allows our ripples to touch others in empowering ways.

Summary

- ✓ Life is like a double-sided puzzle, living with awareness and without.
- ✓ Puzzle pieces from the unaware side have dark colors that give off heavy, unmoving, fearful feelings.
- ✓ The unawareness side of life's puzzles appeals to most people due to its familiarity and fear of change.
- ✓ Puzzle pieces from the awareness side have lighter colors and give off feelings like happiness, joy, and inner peace.
- ✓ In our unawareness we try to control everybody and everything around us.
- ✓ When we come from the awareness point of view, we are clearer on the five-point system.
- ✓ With awareness you are in close contact with your **I Am status.**
- ✓ We can: Do our best, Don't take everything personally, Watch what we say, Don't assume and Forget trying so hard.
- ✓ What we send out will be mirrored back to us
- ✓ Pay attention to how others treat us; this can be a mirror of how we treat others.
- ✓ We are responsible for our own life.

CONCLUSION

By taking full responsibility for yourself, you know now that you can't be responsible for the thoughts, words, actions, and habits of anybody else over the age of seven.

We like to think we are responsible for our children until they leave the house or that it is our job to justify a partner's behavior. We have the impression that other people's behavior is a reflection on ourselves. When our partners or children misbehave or do not react the way we want them to, we feel personally ashamed and ask ourselves how their actions will change other people's opinion of us.

What will "they" say or think? will flow into our thoughts. To make sure that we are not confronted with this shameful feeling we do our best to keep the people around us in check by controlling them to the point that we create guilt or less-than feelings in the people we say we love the most. We often make excuses for the behavior of others. The thought behind that is by helping them, we minimize our feelings of shame and keep everything low-key so that nobody will notice.

If we look at this objectively, the only thing we do is enable the person to continue to have unacceptable behavior. This creates a circle of unwanted behavior and enabling.

The human race started enabling at the same time that romantic love came in the picture. Enabling and unrealistic expectations of love create an idyllic world that needs to appear to be a pink cloud and picture-perfect. This is a fool's world with a herd of nasty elephants in the room - shame, blame, and guilt.

Family and culture teaches us to look after the weaker ones in the world. In the meantime, we have no clue who the "weaker" ones are, because nobody explained that from an empowering perspective. The weaker are seen only as victims. The strongest will survive depending on your perspective.

If you believe strong refers to physical ability: When you have a handicap, you need protection, and we have to feel sorry for you.

Therefore you are less "worthy" because you don't contribute to the community as a whole; you only take up service. You can't think for yourself, so we have to do that for you. It doesn't matter if your handicap

is being blind, deaf, illiterate, or wheelchair-bound, having
no education, or living in a Third World country. You need help, and we will give it to you, with strings attached of course.

If you believe strong refers to mental and spiritual ability: Strength means being resilient to what life challenges come your way and being flexible and adaptable and trusting in your own power.

The strongest person becomes those with strong mental and spiritual abilities. I have met extraordinary people who showed great resilience to the cards that were dealt to them. In the same breath I can say the opposite as well. Some of us will cave under the cards that were dealt to us, and it doesn't matter how strong we physically are.

Bottom line: We need mental and spiritual strength to survive and thrive in this physical world. You can deal with physical limitations when you are mentally and spiritually strong. You understand that you have more than your body's performance abilities to offer the world. You have multiple talents and a willingness to use them. You are a valuable and contributing person to the world at large.

Our thoughts, words, actions, and habits support this statement.

Let's take a look at the ripple effect to see how our actions and habits support what we see happening in the world today:

I Am status: We may or may not be on the same page with our thoughts, words, actions, and habits with what we want to communicate to others.

Family culture: We enable unwanted behaviors by making excuses to avoid blame, shame, and guilt feelings and to keep the family name clean.

Societal culture: The "strong" have to rescue the weaker ones. And the "strong," a.k.a. governments and big corporations, will decide who the weaker ones are and what kind of help they need.

Media culture: Propaganda tells us we need to be physically fit, slim, and strong. If you do not fit the mold, there is something wrong with you, and we will tell you exactly how to fix it.

What would the world look like if we were all standing in our personal power? If we knew that mistakes and failure are great opportunities for learning and that they only represent a chance to deepen our inner power? If we understood that others were on the same discovery path and when they made a mistake or failed, we could respond with compassion and forgiveness, and teach them to do the same for us.

But first we have to take full responsibility for ourselves and refuse to take on responsibilities that are not our own. This is a difficult choice because only you can make that choice for you and those around you. How strong are you mentally and spiritually? That is the question.

Some of the greatest that lived among us showed us how to do it—Jesus, Abraham Lincoln, inventors, Nelson Mandela, Mother Theresa, and Joan of Arc. They taught us not to compromise our own beliefs and truths and while still being of service to the world as a whole. They were human. They failed, they learned, they carried on.

We are as valuable and have the same potential. We have lots to offer. We can choose to believe in ourselves and by extensions in the value of others. We have the same abilities and backgrounds. They were born with their toolboxes and five-point systems just as we are. They listened, knew who they were (their **I Am status**), their Vancouver and the talents they possessed. They had doubt but they took full responsibility for themselves and refused to enable the people around them. It can be done. It is evident around us. We have examples living in our communities, maybe in our homes.

For me, Will and Sue are my two biggest inspirations. They stood in their own personal power and encouraged me to do the same. Will had the ability to get across what and how he wanted things done without making you wrong.

For example, my job was to sweep and clean up behind the bunker silos when I was fifteen. I hated sweeping and did a half-hearted job one day, pushing all the leaves under a tarp. Behind me, Will said with a laugh, "If my dad saw me do that, I would get my ass kicked."

I got the message - we don't do that here. I didn't feel punished, just teased in a way even I could laugh about, but I never do a half-hearted job because I still hear Will's voice in my head.

We are surrounded with inspirations, people who embody those qualities we need to create in ourselves. I know a single mom with two teenagers to raise who doesn't let her abusive childhood stop her from doing the best she can and taking responsibility for herself.

My son got married without a job or place to live and showed me you can do anything when you believe in yourself.

We humans are stronger and more resilient then we believe. When a catastrophe, like a tornado or illness rips apart communities and lives, we not only survive but come together to help.

Although, we are more familiar with our responsibility to the family or group, we are learning about personal responsibility and how to reconcile it with perceived conflicts with family and culture expectations.

Earlier in the book I wrote that when we come from our **I Am status**, we can't hurt anybody on purpose, because we are coming from love. This statement is a good reference for any inner turmoil we experience. When we know a decision is coming from our authentic qualities, we know that it is the best choice for us at that time with the information we have. That does not mean that those around us will not challenge our decision or try to convince use to change our minds.

In the following examples, such conflict can be reconciled with patience, faith in ourselves and not giving into feelings of bitterness or anger.

If we choose a partner that is good for us, despite our parents' objections, it becomes necessary to communicate why this is the right partner choice while being compassionate, kind and listening to the family's viewpoint. It becomes the family members' responsibility to make their choice on what they do. Their actions may include the accepting the chosen partner or rejecting them and losing connection with their child and/or their family member. It is their choice to make. The stronger the family member's stands in their choice, possibly, the quicker a family will come around. And if they don't, the family member has to be strong enough to shoulder this challenging path and keep relating to their family from a loving perspective. Look at the history of intercultural relationships, same-sex relationships, mixed-religion relationships, and diverse social status relationships. Many couples have challenged their upbringing and that of their family's on this matter.

- ✓ Moving away from your family: If one's life path goes outside the family's expectations about where one should live due to beliefs, expectations, neediness or simply that no one else has moved that far away, one's decisions may be questioned and fought. When you feel that moving away is the best decision for you and you communicate that clearly with compassion and empathy, your family should eventually come around if they value your relationship. If not, they hurt themselves by going into a negative spiral, which is not your responsibility.
- ✓ Making a career choice the family is not happy with. When a person's career choice becomes a struggle point for their family, communicating clearly about what makes this career choice important to you is essential. Listen at Level 3 to understand what makes them so apprehensive about your choice. You can't make them like your career choice, but you can try to explain to them in a way that creates a mutual understanding.
- ✓ Using only the family values you feel connected to will always trigger a mirror effect. It may

look as if you feel that you are better than your family. You are the crab in the bucket who wants to crawl out.
- ✓ Choosing your own spiritual path and not blindly following your family's path. You are the one who is questioning if what you learned is true for you. Most of us feel threatened by that kind of confidence. It shows inner strength, and those who are weaker will show signs of envy that can escalate into conflict.

The moment you choose to listen to your inner wisdom, you are standing in your own power. This can be seen as threatening and scary to others, yet in the same breath we feel threatened and scared when we don't stand in our personal power. It is a paradox that most people ignore, and by not facing the paradox, we keep going in circles. It is like the endless question, what came first, the chicken or the egg? How do we break that circle? How can I be true to myself when my family and friends are fighting with me about my personal decisions?

We start with ourselves. By practicing the Chapter 9 exercises, you will start behaving and making decision from your **I Am status** and building on your own inner power. This creates a foundation for the next step - Don't make anyone wrong.

When you are objective and examine a situation from all perspectives, nobody is wrong in a conflict. When you keep in mind that your perspectives are formed by your **I Am status**, five-point systems, family and societal cultures, media culture, and life experiences, you understand that this is also the case for everybody else.

The reason we engage in conflict is often because we want to be heard, to be in control, or to be right. Look again at the examples above. Is that not what it is all about?

What we don't totally understand is the impact the way we deal with conflict has on ourselves and on others. When we dismiss our **I Am status,** we go against our core values. We betray ourselves. By betraying ourselves we build resentment, frustration, resignation, and cynicism within us.

Those traits hurt the people around you, because those emotions find their way into your interactions with others. The outburst of those emotions will happen sooner or later and often in a way nobody expects. They are often triggered by topics or events not even related to the origin of the emotions. This angers those around you, and the cycle starts.

This pattern has gone on for generations. How can we stop the cycle and make sure that we don't pass this behavior to the next generations? Our only option is to change conflict into an open dialogue.

We need to learn healthy conflict. The first step of healthy conflict is to take personal responsibility in every situation, not just when it is convenient for you. With an open mind, observe the situation. By

observing the situation, you are not running away but rising above the emotions to get a better understanding about what is going on. This allows you to try to understand what the other person is reacting to and why. This insight helps you understand the person and their reaction.

If you can be nonjudgmental, you have found the key to an open interaction. Ask powerful questions that start with what, when, and how to understand what the other person believes has happened. This open dialogue allows you to understand, even if the other person cannot be nonjudgmental or ask powerful questions. Although, it would be great if both parties understood this concept and were willing to work from this point of view, this is rarely the case.

Being able to confront conflict in this manner requires mental and spiritual strength. The conflict can be resolved with just one person working the concepts of open dialogue without judgment.

Change ourselves and we change the way we deal with conflict, changes our environment. Instead of falling into the blame game trap and being judgmental without considering all the fact, one can be open and curious about what makes others so mad at you. What do you mirror to people that they don't want to look at in themselves?

Now it time for you to practice all we've talking about by using your inner strength, your **I Am status**, your toolbox and your quest for who you are and why you and others do what you do.

God bless you and your journey in life.

APPENDIX A

My Life Story

Where do you start when telling others your life story? From the day you were born? From later in life? Or even before you were born?

There are not many who start by explaining how their parents grew up and how that had an impact their lives.

I was born and raised in the south of The Netherlands. My paternal grandmother had a difficult and abusive childhood. She was obsessed with creating status for herself because she came from the wrong side of the tracks. My paternal grandfather was a hardworking, honest man who understood his wife's drive for status. My grandmother lost eleven children, two early in life and the rest in miscarriages. My dad was born way too early, but by God's grace he stayed alive. My grandmother had to feed him every two hours and only a couple of drops of milk at a time. Because Grandma had only two living children left, all her attention and focus were channeled to my aunt and father.

When my dad was eight years old, World War II started. My mom was four at that time. My grandparents became involved with the underground and helped many soldiers escape a dreadful fate. At one point when my dad was twelve, sometime in 1944, he and everybody else had to take cover in a bunker because English and German planes were fighting above the town. An English plane went down, and both my grandparents left the bunker to save the pilot's life. Before they left, Grandma turned around and said to the neighbor, "If we don't come back, will you look after my kids?"

This incident had a great impact on my life. My dad already worshiped his mother, and this incident made her a saint in his mind. It also made it impossible for him to face her disapproval for the rest of his life. It is fair to say that many people had scars from the war. My family's scars were the mental and emotional kind.

When we look at the societal culture at that time, it was uncommon for working-class youth to choose what they wanted to do for a career. At the time, your parents told you what you were going to do; you did that and gave your earnings to the family. That left no room to explore your own strengths and weaknesses. You did what they told you to do.

Keep in mind my dad is a very smart man. He went to work when he was twelve years old. When he was in his twenties, he went back to night school to try to get a higher education. My mom started working as well when she was that age. At that time your parents usually found a job for you, and off you went to work.

The hero worship my father had for his mother was unhealthy. He never questioned his parents. His saboteur was very strong and convinced him to miss a chance to further develop himself with secondary education. Without the education, he only qualified for low-paying jobs. The impact on my mom created her scarcity-of-money mindset. Raising six children was not cheap, even in that time. Some of my siblings, including me, adopted her scarcity mindset as a truth.

Dad was smart and though he couldn't prove himself in his job, he volunteered to prove himself and feel like he was accomplishing something important. This was good for his self-esteem but not for us children. He was never home. Mom raised us and was always there. This is how I see and experience my life to this day.

While my father was fighting with his saboteur, I started my life in 1966 with a bang. I came speeding into this world as the fourth of six children. The delivery took only one hour and thirty minutes. I was three weeks early. Some of my family will tell you that

I've never had any patience, right from the beginning. It has taken me a long time to learn patience, but now I can say I have patience.

When I was three, my mom took me to see a girl up the street, and I befriended her immediately. For years I would play there every day. Her mom gave me the attention I didn't receive from my parents. I didn't get much attention because my younger brother was born with spina bifida. He was born when I was five, and I felt the moment he came in the world, I lost my parents. They didn't abandon me by conscious choice, but they went into survival mode to deal with my brother. To make it more complicated a year and a half later my youngest brother was born.

So the little time Mom had to spend with me was even more reduced. Mom was looking after two young children, one of them requiring special attention and many doctors' visits. Dad was struggling to find self-worth.

I was potty trained, could eat and dress myself, so it was easy to fall between the cracks. Mieke's family became a safe haven for me. Mieke's family took me in as one of their own. They were my sanctuary for over eleven years.

My parents were just surviving with two needy young children, one of whom had a challenging medical condition, four older children, and limited money. For the longest time when I looked back at my childhood, I saw one big black hole regarding my family life. It was like a dungeon - scary and smelly with people screaming and me feeling alone.

Since I have started really looking for my truth, those feelings are gone. Instead I feel compassion and empathy for my parents' struggles. What that means for me personally is that when I look back now the heavy scary feelings are gone. Instead my feelings about my childhood are light like a sunlit open field. My childhood didn't change. My perspective did and that changed my feelings about my childhood.

For me the change feels like a miracle. In a previous chapter when I explained about my scarcity of money mindset it was not surprising, because that was what I saw all around me.

My parents, my neighbors, extended family, friends, everybody around me felt like they did not have what they needed to thrive. At that time, the media culture was not as influential as it is today.

What I saw and felt, I believed to be the truth for everyone We were not taught to go after your dreams, reach for the sky or go outside what was accepted as normal. Your goal was to find a good steady job and stick to it.

This belief made my journey more challenging and more fear-filled while I was on that path. But, it never stopped me and it still doesn't.

As long as I can remember I wanted to be a farmer. My family were not farmers. I had no experience with farming, so when I was fourteen I looked for work on farms that were willing to teach me the skills I desired. I found a job with John and Annie. They had no children and no steady help on the farm. They raised sows and heifers. Every Saturday I mucked out the delivery boxes by hand. It was all straw packed, making it heavy, and dirty work. In the afternoon we would do other odd jobs, like moving sows, weaning the piglets, mucking out the heifer straw pack, and getting feed in. We always ended with sweeping the whole farmyard. Before I started working we had even discussed my paycheck.

When my first day of work was done, I received a pay cheque for five dollars. I was disappointed that I hadn't earned more. I was too young and had been taught to not question my elders, so I didn't ask about it. The next week I hoped for a higher pay but it was still the same - five dollars.

I worked for John for three years, and by the end of the third year, I made twenty-five dollars per day. I put up with the pay and didn't ask for more money because he was willing and able to teach me everything he knew about pig farming and raising heifers. He let me experience everything. When we were working together, he would explain why we did things in detail. John might not have paid me much, but he more than made up for it by paying me in paying in knowledge and experience that was priceless to me. John and Annie's imprint will be with me forever. John allowed me to make mistakes. He was always there to point out the mistakes why they were mistakes and how I could learn from them. I never made the same mistake twice.

The second farm I worked at was a dairy farm owned by Will and Sue. I swear to this day that Will and Sue are earth angels. What they taught me was a soul-deep connection to someone and something. They taught how life is great, even when it sucks. Will and Sue had four children, three sons and a daughter. The youngest son was killed when he was three years old in a farm accident. The middle two children ended up with brain damage due to an accident, and they could never live on their own. The oldest son became a teacher but never took over the farm. He died in a car accident, leaving a wife and four children behind.

Will and Sue had a bumpy ride in life. But I can still feel Sue's presence and her calm reassurance that I can do everything that I want to do. In all the years I worked and were friends with them, I never heard them say one swearword, gossip or talk badly about anybody. When I hear the word grace, the picture I get in my head is Will and Sue.

Will taught me how to drive a tractor and what was involved with raising calves and milking cows. I worked with them for over four years and became friends with them. Sue always had time for me and gave me solid feedback on how I could be a better person. It was from them I learned the impact of being non judgmental. I knew that they treated everybody with the same respect, because I saw it repeatedly with every person they met.

When I was fifteen, I met Luke (my husband) at my aunt's place.

While we were on a family holiday with my aunt and her family, my cousins started a friendship with Luke and his friends who were also at the same campground. When Luke and his friends came for a visit, I happened to be at my aunt's place. That's where I saw Luke for the first time. We started talking, and by the end of the visit he promised me to call me. He did.

It took a while, but after lots of phone calls we were in a relationship. It was not easy because we lived an hour and a half from each other. Neither of us had a driver's license. In the beginning, our relationship was all by phone. After a couple of weeks I went to see him at his house. His family owned a dairy farm, and they had finish pigs. I was received with open arms. His parents knew that I wasn't from a farm but that I went to an agricultural school and that my main passion was farming. His parents and I

hit it off from day one. Luke's dad became my dad. He always paid attention to me, and he would pick up on my moods. If I was sad about something or I had something on my mind, he always would ask me about it. Even if I brushed him off, he wouldn't give up. He would just ask calmly again what was wrong. He would do that until I told him what was wrong.

He really was into the soul connection as well. Luke lived on the farm his parents and sister and his grandparents. His grandfather was what you would call a wise man. He knew when he needed to talk and when to listen. So in my life were two more people who taught me to listen in Levels 2 and 3. My life would never be the same.

For the first time I felt unconditionally loved by a family. I recognized it because I had experienced it with Mieke and her family and with Will and Sue. But this was the first time with people I called family. Life was good. I really started to feel that my life was heading in the right direction.

However, my parents didn't hit it off with Luke. It wasn't that they hated him. They didn't think he was treating me well enough. From the day I met Luke I saw only the man he could become. I always encouraged him to do better. I've never met anybody who doesn't have challenges in life. Luke had his own coping mechanisms and they were not always refined.

Looking back, I realize Luke was rude when he got the impression that he had to protect me, and it didn't matter from whom or at what cost. He wasn't possessive, just protective.

So life went on. I had great people in my life and I got an education I was very interested in, despite being bullied in school, where the ratio was 97% guys who never learned how to relate to 3 % of the ladies in attendance. No wonder there was bullying going on.

Luckily I came out unscathed but I can relate to others who were or are experiencing bullying. It is a very disheartening feeling that seems to be getting more violent these days.

When you are young you assume that nothing can bring you down, and that you are invincible. I thought that too, until life taught me a real lesson. After I finished my agriculture education, I was nineteen.

I moved to Luke's farm and lived with his parents, until we built a new addition on the house for us.

On December 9, 1985, I came back from work with back pain. The pain came out of the blue without any indications of the cause. The book will be too long if I go into details, but my life hasn't been the same since. I went from doctor to doctor, and nobody seemed to know what the problem was. I was walking with a cane, bent over like a banana. Lying in bed was where I had the least amount of pain. There were days when I was in so much pain that I would tell people to not even touch the bed. Every movement would vibrate through my body and cause fiery pain.

One day my legs refused to work, so Luke and his dad took me to the hospital. By God's grace the hospital took me in, but they didn't know what to do with me, because my symptoms didn't fit any disease they knew about. I had all the tests done. It looked as if I was suffering from a herniated disk, but they couldn't see anything on the x-ray. This hospital stay happened in year three of my back and leg pain. Because they didn't know what to do, the doctor advised me to see a psychologist. I knew my pain wasn't a fabrication of my mind. There was something wrong with my body. But I had come to a point where I needed to prove to the doctors that my pain was not mental but physical. To do so I had to see a psychologist. I was so fed up that I told them to send a psychologist down.

After two sessions with a psychologist he knew that my problems weren't mental. So I went back to my family doctor, and they sent me to a neurologist in a small hospital. This doctor was willing, ready, and able to look outside the box. He ordered a special kidney test to see the location of my kidneys. He found out that my right kidney hung against my spine when I stood up, and that created the symptoms of a herniated disk.

On April 27, 1989, they operated to fasten the kidney to my lowest rib. My symptoms were greatly lessened after that, but nerve damage had been done.

I saw myself as an independent young woman who knew who she was and what she wanted. Believe me; a situation like that tests your belief system to no end. I started questioning myself. Was my mind creating the back pain? Was I making myself sicker then I really was? Was the pain even real? Did I create the pain just to get attention and sympathy from people? Over those four years I had periods when those questions floated through my mind. In those periods I felt as if I was in a dark space. It was hard to reach me. Not many people could, not even Luke. I would retreat inside myself and hide my desperation behind a thick wall. My face was joyful and fun, but behind my mask I was crying. Almost nobody saw through my mask except my father in-law and our minister. Those two people could hold me in my desperation, and they never disappointed me.

At that time, I didn't know meditation, so all I did to stay sane was pray—not just in church either. I even prayed when I did the dishes. When I prayed, something deep inside me would come to the front and give me strength to believe in myself and that I wasn't making myself sick and that there was something mechanically wrong with me, the doctors only had to find it.

I was not hopeless, even when I felt hopeless, useless, and a burden for Luke and my in-laws. I felt it was my responsibility to heal myself. That meant a lot of doctors and not giving up.

This is the story of my life - to believe in myself at all times.

Most of my life lessons have that in common. While my back pain was going on, Luke and I got married. The day before the wedding I got a cortisone injection in my spine so that I could walk down the aisle. When you look at your ceiling for years alone with your thoughts, you either get to know yourself really well, or you go crazy. I got to know myself really well, and I knew I wasn't mentally unstable. I learned a lot about people and assumptions because I was judged, a lot. That may sound weird. How can you judge a sick person? But when there is no diagnosis, people assume it is all in your head, and they lose patience with you. They stop showing interest and move out of your life. I found out who my real friends were, and there weren't many.

All this time I lived on the farm, and when I could work a little bit, I would help out on the farm. I pushed myself every chance I got. When I was mobile, I would work. At one point we lived with four generations on one farm. In my sick period our oldest son, Adrian, was born. When I was pregnant, the baby kept my kidney in place, so I had fewer problems. My mother in-law helped me a lot with the kids. She would help with the everyday care. You may ask why I would start a family if I wasn't well. Well, we didn't know if I ever would be better, and at that time our parents were still young and willing to help out. That was our motivation to start a family right away.

After my kidney surgery my back pain lessened, so I was more functional. With some restrictions, I could live with that amount of pain without a problem.

When I was pregnant with Paul, our second son, Adrian developed epilepsy. One morning he said his ear was hurting, and he fell down. After a couple of weeks going to the family doctor, not knowing what was wrong, Adrian had a seizure at the doctor's office.

Immediately we were sent to the specialist. Doctor appointment after doctor appointment was on the agenda again, this time for our son. I felt so hopeless, and I wished that I could take on Adrian's illness. Adrian's epilepsy was difficult to regulate. He would have fifteen to twenty seizures a day. Can you imagine what that does to a two-year-old child? Do you know how hard it is to raise a child who is fighting with you all the way because he doesn't understand what is wrong with him? Our family was going in circles with how to raise Adrian and how to regulate his epilepsy. At this point our extended family gave us lots of advice about how to control our son, like "Don't forget what is the best for your child." All good and well, but there were many assumptions, and I felt judged by people who had no experience with a sick child.

Because Adrian was out of control, if I wanted to correct him, he would still laugh at me. After two years of this, I looked at Adrian's doctor and told him I couldn't do this anymore. I was mentally, emotionally, and physically exhausted. The doctor took one look at me and said, "You're right, you can't do it anymore." Two weeks later Adrian was in a special epilepsy clinic. That was the best choice we had ever made, because here Adrian came in contact with other epilepsy patients. Here he found recognition and understood that he was not the only one with a problem.

Every weekend we would pick him up. So one Friday I was there to pick him up, and he was bouncing on the sofa next to me. I looked over, and without thinking I said, "Adrian, get off the couch, and start getting your stuff. Mom will drink her coffee with Nurse Pete, and then we go." When he was gone, Pete looked at me and said that he found it amazing how I was dealing with this situation. He said that other parents were afraid to correct their child because of the possibility they might inflict a seizure on them. I laughed at that and said, "He will get a seizure anyway whatever I say or do, and when he is fifteen, I will still be the boss in my house and not my children." Pete replied, "Yes, you are right, and I'm very happy to see that you think like that. I wish that all parents did that."

When Adrian was in this clinic, I found out that I was pregnant again, with baby number three. This pregnancy was difficult from day one. I was nauseated before my period stayed away. I would vomit at least four times a day, and when I was nineteen weeks pregnant, I started to get contractions. Adrian came home from the clinic on March 27, and I went into the hospital on April 17. After two weeks everything seemed to calm down, and I went home.

Only a couple of days later my water broke when I was twenty-one

weeks. When we discovered that, the doctor didn't give us any hope the baby would survive. We started talking about a funeral for our baby. They even sent me home and told me to come back if labor started and to call the family doctor if that was not possible. When I reached twenty-five weeks, they took me into the hospital, awaiting the birth. I spent another nine and a half weeks in the hospital before our son Peter was born. This was another test for my mental strength and our marital relationship.

In every situation a message of hope is sent to you. In my case it came from a woman I met in the hospital. She had a very, very difficult delivery, and on the day I was transported to a special hospital, she came to say good-bye and wished me luck. She also gave me a rose from her own bouquet. For her it maybe was a small thing, but for me it was huge. For me it represented hope. When I think of this rose, I still feel warmth toward that lady, and she probably has no idea how much this gesture meant to me.

To navigate my sickness, Adrian with epilepsy, Paul developing asthma, and a risky pregnancy is not for the faint of heart. And if that doesn't stretch your relationship, I don't know what will. During this time, we were also running a dairy farm.

Even if our relationship was tested to the limit, Luke and I kept connecting and supporting each other the best we could. Sometimes that meant a lot of talking, screaming, and sometimes silence between us. In this time my father in-law came down with a herniated disk and needed surgery.

Normally he, Luke, and I ran the farm, but now it was only Luke available to look after the farm. But with me gone and two little boys at home that was not an easy task. How we ever did all this is still a miracle to me. We were confronted with very difficult living situations that had a tremendous impact on each of us personally and on us as a couple. Dealing with health issues in all different shapes and forms from the time I was eighteen shaped me and Luke as people. What made it more difficult was living with four generation on one farm, because we had a business together and were family living in the same space. There were some periods of conflict, but we always could talk about it, and when we were done talking, it was never brought up again. Not a day after nor a year later—done was done. I have seen that played out in other ways in different families.

In 1991 Luke and I went to Canada on a trip. This trip changed our lives forever. It was an organized trip from flight to hotels to activities. We landed in

Toronto, and while we were driving north to Kingston, we fell in love with Canada. I loved everything I saw, heard, and smelled. When we came back, the family asked us how it was, and we said it was great and we wanted to live there. Believe me, the parents weren't impressed. This was all in the midst of Adrian's epilepsy and Paul's asthma, and shortly after we came home I was pregnant with Peter. So the first couple of years after the trip we had other priorities to deal with, but Canada was not out of my mind. I felt homesick for the wide open spaces, less traffic, and a less hectic way of living. So after five years, when everything with the kids was going in the right direction, I came to a point where I couldn't suppress those homesick feelings any longer. It was time to look into the immigration process.

It took us two years, lots of phone calls, testing Adrian in Canada, and great help from our doctor who did the medical papers for the Canadian government to get the visas. This was another point in our lives when we had to keep the faith that we would make it. We knew that others got their visas in six months, so yeah, we needed to believe because not living in Canada was not an option. Again our faith came through, and on July 29, 1998, we got our visas in the mail. We were over the moon.

We became Canadian landed immigrants on September 10, 1998.

Now it was my little family "alone" in this big world with no backup, no family we could call to help out when things were difficult. The children didn't speak English but learned quickly. In this new country we encountered challenges we had never had to face before. It started when we built the new barn. Cow health was declining, and the milk production went down. After years of frustration and switching feed companies we had it somewhat under control but not totally. Then we found out we had stray voltage in the barn. You hear more about that in North America than in Europe, and it devastates and cripples you.

Europe has a different electricity system than North America, and that is where the problems lie. When it is present, it effects the milk production, the animals' health, and the reproduction ability of the cows. All these factors can be translated affect the bottom line of the farm account. Stray voltage is not something you can see, smell, touch, or taste, and most of us can't feel it. Cows can. To fight this unseen enemy is a difficult task.

Are we out of the woods yet? We're getting there, but now there's new challenges on the horizon due to a huge wind farm that is being built around the farm. The future will tell the impact they have on our dairy operation. People underestimate the mental and emotional strain this has on a farm family. We all want to succeed in our business, but when things go south and you can't see what you need to fight against, it puts enormous pressure on the managers.

For myself this was another attack on my beliefs. I came to the conclusion that my self-worth was coupled with the farm's bottom line. So the better the farm did financially, the better and more worthy I was. Therefore, in reverse, because we seemed unable to get out of this downward spiral, I felt lazy, not smart enough, not a good manager, awful with money, and not worthy to farm. To say my saboteur was in control was putting it mildly. In this period God sent me a new messenger, Jim. He understands energies in all shapes and forms, and he was one of the people who helped us to get the stray voltage under control.

He also made me realize my curiosity about my life question, what makes people do the things they do? Through him I wanted to do something for others and make a difference in somebody else's life. So I started volunteering in the juvenile system and at a youth correction center. I did different things there, and my favorite was a discussion group with five young men, all around seventeen years of age. We would meet once a week for two hours, and we would talk about anything except hair, makeup, and fashion. The rest was fair game. We talked all right. I learned just as much as the guys did. When we started, I told them, "You don't have to agree with what I say, the good Lord gave you brains, so use them."

One by one they were released, and when one left, he told me, "Ellen, I didn't always agree with you, but boy, did you make me think." I may have taught those young men to think for themselves, but they have taught me a lot too, especially how to walk in somebody else's shoes. I remember one incident when we were talking about love. This 6'4" seventeen-year old shared with me that he didn't know how love felt. Right at that moment my heart broke for him, and I saw his **I Am status** coming out.

I decided to do an exercise where they had to sit with their backs to me and pen and paper in hand. I would think of an emotion, and they had to write down what they thought the emotion was. He got them all, so at least he knew now what love felt like. I'm so blessed to have met those young men. They taught me how incredible humans are. They all have a special place in my heart. I wish them all the best.

So how did I go from being a dairy farmer to a certified co-active coach? Well, due to my volunteering in the correction center and as a scout leader I became more certain that I wanted to teach people communication skills and how to connect to their **I Am status**. My first thought was to become a social worker. This would give me the credentials and authority to help others who were in need. But as I thought about it, the less appealing it became. In my mind, as a social worker, you put people in a box, and the help you provide depends on which box the person is in. For me personally that is not my way of working. I wanted to be free to empower everyone by asking powerful questions and by connecting people to their wonderful toolboxes. This way I would get to know amazing people who would become strong. I wouldn't feed the victim. I would feed the powerful **I Am status.** That was why I became a life coach, to see and help others bloom.

Of course my life continues, and every day something new happens. In the summer of 2014 I went back and forth to the hospital again with symptoms of TIA (mini strokes) and hemiplegic migraines. My body keeps me informed on what it needs. This can be rest or being moved to a healthier environment. But that is not the most important thing. I'm still happily married with Luke and have a great relationship with my sons and their partners. I'm already a grandma twice and have wonderful friends. I've moved to a great new house, and to top it off I have to live comfortably. What else in life could I want?

My life was not always a bouquet of roses, but I discovered due to my life experiences - Life is great, even when it sucks.

APPENDIX B

Real-Life Stories

To conquer fear ... by Marike

I am a fearful woman ... or so I thought. But slowly I've started to realize that maybe I was braver than I gave myself credit for. Slowly I've come to the insight that what was keeping me back all those years were not my own fears but the fears of those around me. To explain how this played out in my personal life, I will tell you the story of my life.

Born second of six and being the eldest girl, my life was about conforming to fixed gender roles and expectations. As a young girl I loved to read, but I was told I could spend my time better helping out my mum with housework. I was expected to mind and care for the younger children whenever we were home alone, but my elder brother was the one praised for being in charge. I loved school and wanted to study but was sent to a lower-level secondary school because I was expected to get married and wouldn't need to provide for a family. This mix-up between what I wanted and what was expected made me question myself and my abilities, and I grew fearful of not being good enough, afraid of stepping out of line, and anxious to fit in and be "a good girl."

After graduation I started nursing, but that wasn't a success either, as my priorities were slightly different from those of my superiors. Also, I found it hard to deal with the stress that nursing brings, and I was only seventeen, too young for a job this hard. Then I joined the air force ... The military might not seem the right place for someone who is fearful, and yet there I was enjoying (most of) it, and I was good at my job!

I felt ready for a relationship but not with someone from work, so I placed an ad in the personal section of the paper, and I met a wonderful man. I started to become even braver and bolder in my life choices—not because he gave me permission but because he saw what I couldn't see; I was more fearless than fearful. Within five years of meeting him we were married, bought a house, and had two children.

At nearly thirty I craved finally going to college, and with his support I could do so, even if I didn't have the level of education needed for a degree course. I wanted to study theology, and when I received my course material, I was in shock. Not only was it daunting to embark on this journey of college education, but also the list of subjects was complete abracadabra to me! It took me a few years, but I did get a degree (oh, and a third child in the middle of all that). Although my husband was very supportive, I was questioned by many, including the rest of my family, or at least my sanity was. Who was to look after my children when I was in college (their father)? What would people think of a mother who abandoned her children on the weekend for her own enjoyment? How could I start a college degree after having had two children? What would studying theology do to my faith? And then it got even worse ...

In 2000, as I was due to finish my master's degree, my husband and I decided that we wanted to immigrate to Ireland, a decision made almost overnight. We put our house up for sale, packed up our belongings, took the children out of school, and my husband quit his job. Just before we were due to leave there was still much uncertainty about whether we had a place to live or a job for my husband, but we pushed through anyway. Our families found it hard to understand why we would want to do this, and although they tried to be as supportive as they could, they expressed some doubts. How will you cope all on your own? What are you doing to your children? What about the religious tensions in Ireland? And my absolute favorite: What does this move mean to your pension plan?

Only a week before we left we found a house and a job, so all was well. To start a new life in another country means cutting ties with your family, friends, home country, and everything that is familiar to you. As there is nothing and nobody to fall back on, you have to depend on yourself and each other. At first I was a stay-at-home mum, doing school runs, helping out at school, and making sure that the children settled into this new life. But quite soon I was asked to teach religion to a group of teenagers in an experimental secondary school and to write all the material for this class. I took the leap and taught religion for a few years. I also assisted in the handwork classes, and after the handwork teacher retired, I became the new handwork teacher.

For a long time it had been my wish to become a celebrant, and in the back of my head there was this niggling voice that insisted I finally finish my master's degree in order to do so. As no Irish university offered a master's course that appealed to me, I started a course at the University of Wales. Doing a distance master's degree in a language that is not your own, teaching classes, and raising a family all at the same time is challenging to say the least. In the end I did not complete the degree, as I took too long to complete my modules. When I got the news that I couldn't continue, I was devastated for about a day.

Then I got mad and decided that I would do it anyway. I drew up a vision plan and a business plan, wrote articles, made up advertisements, and started a new business that is now really starting to take off. Looking back over my life so far, I can see that I am fearless, or at least not as timid and fearful as I always thought I was. Together with my husband as well as on my own, I have made some bold decisions, ventured off the beaten track, taken some turns that didn't work out, fallen flat on my face, and gotten back on my feet again. What made me fear life was not my own trepidation but that of others. It was when people, well-meaning as they were, questioned my desires and decisions. It was they who feared me stepping out of line and doing things they were afraid to do; they tried to keep me back by making me doubt my actions. And

I have realized one thing: not only am I stronger than I thought, but I am also much, much braver than I ever dared imagine.

Jozien's Story

I grew up being the fourth of five siblings on a farm in the Netherlands. I had a good life with friends close by. They were a couple of years older than me and therefore also went to school a couple of years earlier. At elementary school things didn't always go so well, and because of that I many times felt inferior to other people. I have a brother two years older than me who had to go to a school for children with learning difficulties after elementary school. I have a younger sister who also went to such a special school because she couldn't learn so well. My older brother and sister could learn better and went to the lower general secondary school. I was a bit jealous of them because I felt they could learn better than I could. I felt I was somewhere in between my brothers and sisters. I went to the domestic science school, and over there things went so well that I made the switch to the same school as my older brother and sister. At the time of the final exams I had so much exam anxiety that I quit school. At that time I was sixteen and started working, first at a greengrocer, later in a liquor store where I also did some housekeeping, after that in a bakery, and finally at a home-help organization.

During that time I had many boyfriends, some short-term, others a while longer. And then I met

Joost. He was such a calm and interesting guy, and many times he made me laugh. We quickly got to know each other very well because he already lived by himself.

After having a relationship of only a year we knew we wanted to get married and buy a house. When I had my first baby, a girl, I quit my job and became a full-time mother. I did this for eight years until my youngest child turned four and went to school. I have always been happy that I could raise our children myself; I wouldn't have wanted it differently.

The first time I had depression was when we went through a major renovation of our house. Our second child, also a girl, was only six months old and the oldest was two years old. I was overwhelmed so much, and then I also had these hormones jumping around in my body. At the beginning I didn't know what was happening to me. Every morning I had to throw up and couldn't eat a bite. My husband also didn't know what was happening and was fully engaged in the renovation and his job. At a certain point he said that we needed to see a doctor because of my problems. The doctor gave me medication for my depression, but it took a while before the medication started to work. Meanwhile the reconstruction approached its final stage, and that also made me feel better. I was so happy that

I could leave this depressing period behind me and was able to function normally again.

It took us three years before we got our third child, a boy. When I was pregnant with him, I quit the medication a while because it was better for the baby. While pregnant I always really felt good, and there were never signs of feeling depressed. After our son was born I continued to feel good and didn't need the antidepressants anymore.

At the time we had another renovation of the house, and we worked with a very fine constructor. He kept us posted with everything he was about to do and made a good plan and overview of the progress of the reconstruction.

Despite his good planning I was still afraid of going through another depression, so our doctor prescribed medication again for me. This went well for many years until my oldest children were in the fourth and fifth grade of the higher secondary school. They did so well at school that I got that inferior feeling again that I had had in elementary school. This and some other causes made me go through a deep personal crisis, and I had to see our doctor again. He sent me to a psychiatrist. Looking back, this psychiatrist wasn't the best solution for me because all he did was ask how I felt and what his prescribed medication did for me.

He never asked for the root causes of my problems. If I knew then what I know now, I would have found someone to talk with me about what really caused my problems. A psychiatrist is not suited for that, but we didn't know that back then. Looking back, our doctor had to teach that to us. So this psychiatrist's solution was to raise the level of my medication, and he also told me that it could take a while before I would feel better and that it might even become worse for a short while before it would get better.

Well, the result was that I went into a psychosis and thought that ending my life was the solution. This thought made me feel happy because I saw a way out of this miserable feeling. My solution was to take all my medications at once and then drive against a tree.

This way I wouldn't feel anything anymore and would not be a burden anymore for my family.

Indeed I drove against a tree, but as if saved by an angel, I had almost no injuries. This was probably also caused by all the antidepressants I had in my body, which relaxed my body in the way alcohol does when you are drunk. I was taken to the hospital and later transferred to a special psychiatric department of the hospital. I stayed there for three months. Together with my husband I have learned a lot over there. Another person who was very valuable to me was my new psychologist who did an IQ test with me. This test showed me that I was more intelligent than I thought and that my level of education was at the same height as my older brother and sister.

Later at home I had to earn the right of being a trustworthy mother and wife again. If I wanted to do shopping, at first someone always went with me, as my family was afraid in the beginning of leaving me alone. At first they were always afraid that I might do something to myself again. Later on that got better and better. I also lost my driver's license for a year because of the car accident. Together with my family and people close to me I have been fighting to get through this difficult time. Fortunately I've come out of this terrible experience even stronger. Nowadays our two dogs also help me in lesser times. My husband says that you always need to have something to wish for and should strive to do things better in life. That is what I am trying to do now, and I am convinced that it will continue to go well in my life.

Joost

When a human is born, he or she has certain qualities by birth. These can be properties like joyfulness, curiosity, being spontaneous, being quiet, being active, or so on. In the course of your life you are exposed to all kinds of outside influences. These can be positive and can let the qualities you are born with grow. For many people, though, their innate qualities are suppressed; many layers of properties that impede mental growth and development are laid over the innate qualities.

If people want to work on personal development, they first need to become aware of who they really are, who other people really are, and why they are the way they are. Only if you have discovered this and are aware of it can you start working on yourself. At that point you will learn to have more respect, not only for other people but also for yourself. You have to respect yourself in that you are just the way you are right now. By living the life you have lived so far, you have become exactly the person you are now.

You then don't need to blame yourself for why you are the way you are. When you have accepted this and are conscious of this fact, only then can you wonder if you are satisfied with who you are right now. It may be that you are okay with it, and that's fine. After all, it's your life! It is also possible that you are not satisfied with your current life. At that moment you have a chance to start working on yourself the right way. It's going to be, as they sometimes say, "the first day of the rest of your life." You then have a zero point; this is who you are right now. This is your baseline so far, and you need to accept it the way it is now. Starting today, you can work on who you want to be. You can then go back to your roots, your childhood, and who you were before other people and society started influencing you. That is your toolbox. Below I have elaborated this for myself.

Who was I in my early childhood? What was my toolbox?

After examining my early childhood I found that I was an open personality, a cheerful, optimistic, curious, sensitive, empathic, and resilient person. What did I become later in my life? I became a silent, uncertain person who thought that other people's opinions were more important than mine. I felt attacked quickly, and I had no perseverance. I grew up as the youngest of a large family of seven children. On one hand, by being the youngest, I was relatively free, and there was not much pressure on me from the family. On the other hand, being the youngest, my opinion was mostly determined by the rest of the family. As I grew older, I started noticing more and more of the dominant character of my father. Mainly he decided what would happen in our family. Actually his character had two sides. On one hand he was always consistent; for everyone he applied the same firm rules, and in his way he meant the best for all of us. On the other hand he was also very selfish; everyone had to adapt to him, and sometimes he was unreasonable in that perspective.

Mainly because of this selfish side of my father, I had to protect myself mentally, and that resulted in becoming more and more a closed person, afraid of being hurt over and over. Also because of that selfish side of my father, he clamped down every comment or counterargument, which led to me being submissive to him, not standing up for my own opinion, and therefore always going along with other people's opinion because in my mind other people's opinion were more important than mine.

Being a happy and optimistic person by nature, I somehow was always able to cope with that fact. Despite the many times he pushed me down, I never became a negative or depressed person. On the other hand, my openness, resilience, and curiosity were almost gone.

Because I've always been an empathy, I was many times able to sense without knowing why people like my father subconsciously did what they did. Somehow I knew they just couldn't act differently than the way they did. Later I learned that this came from their own upbringing and development. If no one teaches you how to deal with these characteristics, let alone improve them, it actually makes sense that they've become like this. At moments, when my father had less influence on me, some good characteristics, though sometimes limited, surfaced. My mother stimulated this as much as possible. My mother had a very different character from my father; she was mainly gentle, cooperative, and stimulating. My father often hampered her in these character traits. She, like so many women at that time, thought she had to be subservient to her husband.

At the KPJ (a Dutch youth organization) I had good times when I was away from my dad. I was a lot less bothered by the depressing influences of home and as a result experienced more fun in a lot of things again. At a certain moment I was even asked to become a coach, something my mother encouraged instantly. Yet I mainly remained a closed person; it was a difficult period in my life. Puberty had just started for me, which on its own was already confusing enough. Along with that, the negative impulses from home continued to bother me.

It was only when I fell in love with someone that I got back some of my openness. The girlfriend I then had was someone who really cared about me, something I had experienced only with my mother.

In addition, her family situation was very different from mine. There, people were much more open than at my home, and the children could also stand up for themselves more.

I learned a great deal from that time. Looking back, I restarted developing my natural qualities then. Yet at that time I still was completely unaware of who I really was and what I really wanted in life. My girlfriend at that time was way ahead of me in developing these qualities, and partly because of that, our relationship ended. Around that time a lot of things changed in my life. Besides the fact that my relationship with my girlfriend was over, I got a new job where I had to work alone a lot, I started living on my own, and my mother died unexpectedly. Because of that I was really thrown back and personally went through a deep valley. Without me knowing, one of my natural qualities started developing strongly, and that was my perseverance.

Despite all my personal problems I was able to continue with my life and even came out stronger because of my perseverance. This perseverance has helped me many times throughout life when I've encountered setbacks.

At that same time I got a new girlfriend, Jozien, whom I am still married to today. She helped a lot to get me through this difficult time and helped me regain meaning in my life. She also helped me develop some of my other natural qualities like my joyfulness, curiosity, and optimism. Looking back, some of the not-so-good qualities I developed during my childhood still remained, like being a closed person and not standing up for my opinions and standpoints. My opinions and standpoints were dependent on Jozien's opinions because I was used to doing that and I had never learned or dared to develop my own opinions. This was very difficult for Jozien because she always had to take the lead in our new family that was being formed.

At that time we had three children, two girls and a boy. She also brought in her own development from childhood and wasn't always able to cope with the challenges that came along with raising a young family. During that time, I was very self-occupied because I was slowly becoming aware of who I really was and what my personal problems were. Because of that I didn't see that Jozien was getting into more and more troubles herself, and during a large reconstruction of our house she even went into a depression. I had never experienced such a thing and as such didn't know what was happening, let alone how to cope with it. The causes of Jozien's depression were probably a combination of the reconstruction, the little moral support I was able to give her in raising our young family, and some hormonal problems caused by an unrecognized postnatal depression. She went to the doctor for her problems, and with the help of medication she got back on her feet again. Jozien has used medication ever since. It took me a number of years after this period in our lives to become aware that I even had all these problems; I simply didn't know I had them. It was part of who I was, my normal me at that time. Because I didn't know I had problems, I wasn't able to start working on them.

An important turning point in my life was the moment I heard that my best friend, Ellen, because of her developing spirituality, was able to see and feel things an average person was not able to see and feel. I had heard of people having these capabilities, but that someone so close to me had them as well was an eye-opener to me. I wanted to know more about this, partly because I had become more aware of my own self and my problems.

Ellen recommended I read some books about these subjects like *The Life You Were Meant to Live* by Dan Millman and *The Anatomy of the Soul* by Caroline Myss. These books gave me a start in the exploration of my self. Since then I have read several more books about these subjects and started to apply the thing I've learned in everyday life. This has helped me to slowly develop myself personally and regain my natural qualities.

At the time Jozien and I married we raised a traditional kind of family for that time. I continued to work, and Jozien stopped her job to raise the kids. For her this was her most important task. In the years after, our kids grew up and developed themselves more and more and became less dependent on us. Because it was Jozien's most important task until then, she didn't develop herself further personally. She was more worried about the development of our kids than her own development. Her purpose and task was raising and developing our kids; she also got the most joy out of that.

When that task became less important, Jozien fell into a hole that she suddenly had to fill with something else. Our children also started with a higher education than she had ever had. Two things happened to Jozien because of this. A void emerged that she didn't know how to cope with, and she felt some kind of inferiority when our kids developed themselves further than she had ever done herself. This in combination with a big personal setback we both had in our amateur drama association made Jozien fall into a deep crisis that resulted in her going to the psychiatric department of the hospital. Jozien wasn't capable anymore of taking care of our family, and suddenly that all fell to me. Because I had always put myself in a dependent position toward Jozien, I faced a big problem. How was I supposed to handle all this? Because I already had been busy with personal development for a while, I remembered some of my natural qualities, and at that moment, when it was really necessary, they started floating to the surface by themselves.

I became again that open and optimistic person whom I had been when I was a little child. Also, because I had always been very well able to sense people and had learned to be perseverant, I was able to take over the task of caring for our family from Jozien and lead our family through this crisis. Because of my openness I gave others the opportunity to be able to help us. What you see many times is that people do want to help but are not able to, because they are not given the handles they need from the person who needs help. Thanks to the help we received that way, we were able to remain strong and come out of this crisis so well.

After this crisis I kept developing myself and have become a support for other people more and more. I was also able to develop myself further in my job, which ultimately led to the managing job I have today. All the things that happened to us don't mean that my family or I don't have problems anymore, but we now do have a sufficient toolbox to handle those problems. Sometimes when life takes its daily routine, I sometimes unconsciously slip into a lesser period. What makes the difference now is that I recognize it sooner and am better equipped to handle problems.

PS: Just by writing this story things got even clearer for me than they were before. I wasn't fully aware of all the things we had gone through. It's amazing to see what you are able to achieve when your natural toolbox sets things in motion. I am very grateful that I was given the chance in life to achieve all the things I have achieved. You could say it's a pity that in order for me to come this far we had to go through all the troubles we did. But then again, is it a pity?

APPENDIX C

Below you will find the blank survey questions you may use to find out for yourself how you view the Five-Point System.

Between reading the book and doing the survey, you may discover where your insecurities are located. This awareness will give you a good starting point for connecting more to your **I Am status.**

Filling out the survey is easy. You'll need a pen and some paper (or a journal if you normally journal). Check off the option that applies to you. This can be any or all of the answers and also "other." When you check "other," please give yourself the time to contemplate this question and write the answer in your journal or on a piece of paper. This gives you the chance to revisit your answer at a later date. Remember this is not a test—you can't do this wrong. Just have fun with it.

Q1:   For me, to forgive someone is to

    o   just "forget" all the things the other person did to me even if they really hurt me

- let go of resentment and anger
- try and separate between the person and the thing he/she did that hurt me
- other: feel free to write about that in your journal

Q2: How do you react when conflict arises?

- I act defensively.
- I pretend nothing is happening and hope it blows over.
- I turn inward and refuse to speak to the other person, sometimes for hours or even days.
- I try to stay calm and not take it personally.
- I immediately launch into a counterattack.
- Other.

Q3: Does your reaction to conflict changes within different relationships say mom/partner or strangers?

- Yes.
- No.
- If yes, how? Write about it in your journal.

Q4: What is the biggest challenge you face in any relationship?

- o Listening and feeling listened to.
- o Dealing with conflict.
- o Staying calm when I'm under pressure.
- o Not taking everything so personally.
- o Other.

Q5: What is the effect on you when you decide to go against your family's or friends' wishes?

- o I shut down and forget all about my dreams.
- o I feel insecure and hesitate to proceed.
- o I take my family and friends concerns into consideration but will (in the end) trust my gut feeling.
- o Other.

Q6: How do you pursue your goals?

- o I make a plan and follow the plan to the letter.
- o I make a plan and follow it with a sense of humor.
- o I don't make a plan, and I take opportunities as they come along.

- o Goals? What goals? I have only dreams.
- o Other.

Q7: How do you see yourself when you are held accountable for your actions?

- o I take full responsibility for all my actions.
- o Most of the time events happen, and I just react to them.
- o Other.

Q8: How do you react when peers comment on your performance and behavior?

- o I tune them out.
- o I have a conversation about the comment.
- o I do everything possible to avoid a conversation.
- o I don't want to damage the relationship, so I brush over this conversation.
- o Other.

Q9: How often do you assume that you know what other people think and do (particularly close family and friends)?

- I never assume because I know my people.
- I sometimes assume.
- I assume more times then I realize.
- I realize that I'm always assuming till somebody is telling me what they think and feel.
- I do not realize that I'm assuming.
- Other.

Q10: What makes you feel happy and smile?

- My job.
- My family.
- My friends.
- Coffee from my favorite coffee shop.
- Sunshine.
- People smiling.
- Fall weather.
- Other.

Q11: When you hear the word commitment, what comes to mind?

- Making decisions.
- Always making the right decisions.
- Needing to know all the angles to make a decision.

- o I need to trust first before I commit to something.
- o Other.

Q12: What does it take for you to trust another person?

- o My need to feel safe.
- o My need to feel heard.
- o My need to feel understood.
- o Feeling like I can be myself.
- o Other.

Edwards Brothers Malloy
Oxnard, CA USA
September 4, 2015